Better Homes and Gardens®

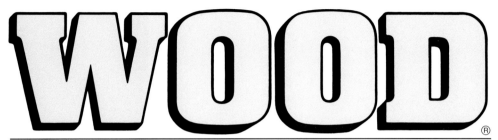

WOOD®

GUIDE TO

SETTING UP YOUR SHOP

All of us at Meredith® Books are dedicated to giving you the
information and ideas you need to create beautiful and useful
woodworking projects. We guarantee your satisfaction with this
book for as long as you own it. We also welcome your comments
and suggestions. Please write us at Meredith® Books, RW-240,
1716 Locust St., Des Moines, IA 50309-3023.

A **WOOD** BOOK
Published by Meredith Books

MEREDITH BOOKS
President, Book Group: Joseph J. Ward
Vice President and Editorial Director: Elizabeth P. Rice
Executive Editor: Connie Schrader
Art Director: Ernest Shelton
Prepress Production Manager: Randall Yontz

WOOD MAGAZINE
President, Magazine Group: William T. Kerr
Editor: Larry Clayton

GUIDE TO SETTING UP YOUR SHOP
Produced by Roundtable Press, Inc.
Directors: Susan E. Meyer, Marsha Melnick
Senior Editor: Marisa Bulzone
Managing Editor: Ross L. Horowitz
Graphic Designer: Leah Lococo
Design Assistant: Betty Lew
Art Assistant: Polly King
Proofreader: Amy Handy

For Meredith Books
Editorial Project Manager/Associate Art Director: Tom Wegner
Contributing How-To Editor: Marlen Kemmet
Contributing Techniques Editor: Bill Krier
Contributing Tool Editor: Larry Johnston
Contributing Outline Editor: David A. Kirchner

Special thanks to Khristy Benoit

Meredith Corporation Corporate Officers:
Chairman of the Executive Committee: E. T. Meredith III
Chairman of the Board, President and Chief Executive Officer:
  Jack D. Rehm
Group Presidents: Joseph J. Ward, Books; William T. Kerr, Magazines;
  Philip A. Jones, Broadcasting; Allen L. Sabbag, Real Estate
Vice Presidents: Leo R. Armatis, Corporate Relations;
  Thomas G. Fisher, General Counsel and Secretary;
  Larry D. Hartsook, Finance; Michael A. Sell, Treasurer;
  Kathleen J. Zehr, Controller and Assistant Secretary

On the front cover: Labor-of-Love Workbench, pages 47–55
On the back cover: The Ultimate Router Fence System, pages 72–75;
  Great Organizers for Your Shop Tools, pages 28–34

SHOP ORGANIZERS YOU CAN MAKE

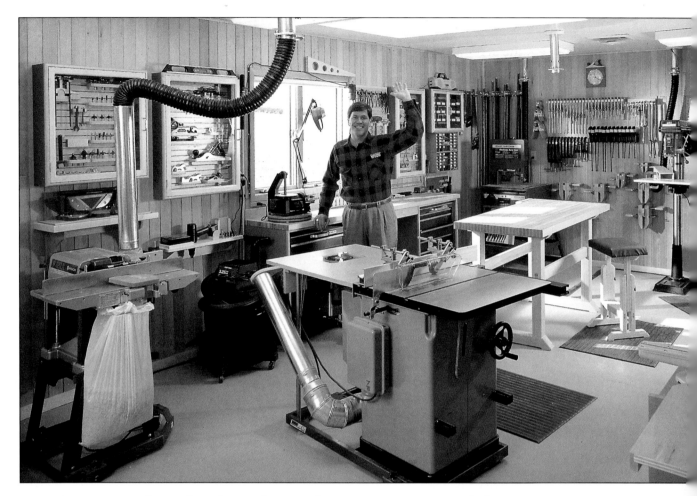

Here's your guide to the shop of your dreams! From a workshop
we've remodeled from the ground up to organizers and holders
for all of the most popular tools, our plans will put every item
you need within reach right when you want it.

HERE IT IS! *WOOD*® MAGAZINE'S IDEA SHOP™

You say you want some help planning a new workshop? Or maybe you've got the urge to reorganize the one you have now. Either way, you've come to the right place. During your tour of *WOOD*® magazine's all-new Idea Shop™, you'll discover how we took a 14×28' bare-bones room and remodeled and outfitted it into the sensational, feature-filled woodworking center shown. Use any of the ideas you like—after all, we built this shop just for you.

Welcome, woodworkers, to *WOOD*® magazine's Idea Shop™. It's the result of almost a year of space planning, project designing, construction, and installation by nearly everyone on the staff. But was it ever worth spending time and energy!

As you might imagine, we took a lot into consideration when we sat down at the drawing board to plan this sizable undertaking. We looked at space organization, the working environment, comfort and health features, and, of course, safety and security.

All in all, the Idea Shop™ has turned out to be exactly that—a shop bursting with great ideas. On the following pages, we'll introduce you to the detailed plans and instructions for the super storage units and organizers.

—Larry Clayton
Editor

Like most woodworkers, when we decided to set up the Idea Shop™, we turned to space available. That was an unfinished 14×28' room sharing the same roof with a two-car garage. A room that size compares to many basement bays and measures a little larger than a single-car garage.

As you can see, *WOOD*® magazine's Idea Shop™ *opposite* is packed with some pretty nifty features, such as a concealed dust-collection system with drops, plenty of natural and fluorescent lighting, adaptable storage projects you can build, and lots, lots more. *Above:* The Idea Shop™ exterior.

Even though 14×28' sounds like a lot of space, fitting a full complement of stationary power tools into the room was challenging. (See the floor plan *below* for how we situated our tools.) Note that we located the air-handling *continued*

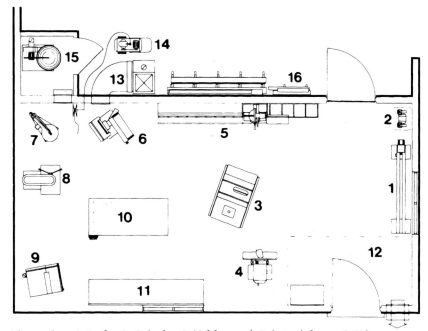

Floor-plan. **1. Lathe 2. Grinder 3. Tablesaw 4. Jointer/planer 5. Mitersaw 6. Belt sander 7. Scrollsaw 8. Drill press 9. Bandsaw 10. Assembly workbench 11. Stationary workbench 12. Finishing area 13. Heating/cooling unit 14. Compressor 15. Dust collector 16. Lumber/sheet-goods storage.**

HERE IT IS! *WOOD*®
MAGAZINE'S IDEA SHOP™
continued

In line with the workstation concept, the sliding compound mitersaw hugs a wall on its own cabinet. The sander, though, sports a mobile base. Note the dust-collection system's drops.

equipment, dust-collection unit, air compressor, and our lumber-storage bin outside of the shop to conserve space, and for other reasons you'll learn about.

Workstations for big tasks

The sliding compound mitersaw station, shown *above,* sees a lot of action, so we built blade and jig storage above for it and for the tablesaw, too. We also added a cabinet-length table extension and fence, and made a handy pullout scrap bin beneath the saw. Other compartments hold portable electric tools, such as routers, drills, and sanders. And there's plenty of storage below.

Continuing the workstation concept, cabinets near the lathe, shown *opposite, top right,* hold turning tools and protective equipment such as a face shield and respirator. There's also related storage near the drill press, bandsaw, and scrollsaw.

The use of solid hemlock tongue-and-groove paneling over drywall creates a warm, inviting look throughout the Idea Shop™. In fact, it contributes to the workstation concept, too. How can that be? The solid wood actually comes in handy for hanging lighter storage units— you don't always have to seek out the studs for a solid anchor. But when it came to hanging the heavy

tool cabinets or other organizers, we relied on wall studs for support.

Controlling the climate

A shop that's too cold or too hot can take the fun out of woodworking. That's why, for winter heating, we went with a 50,000 Btu Lennox gas furnace installed in the adjacent two-car garage, a few feet behind the wood-storage rack. For summer cooling, a companion compressor sits outside.

By locating the furnace in a separate room, we placed a protective wall between the pilot light and any shop-generated dust and volatile fumes. We took a second precaution by installing a 4"-thick pleated filter inside the furnace's cold-air return.

Our battle for clean air

We zeroed in on controlling dust with the addition of a 2-hp collector. It, too, went into available garage space. But, to provide additional dust and noise protection, we housed the collector in its own insulated closet.

Enclosing the dust collector actually accomplishes two things: a) its buildup of exhaust air (containing fine dust particulates) can reenter the shop clean via a filtered vent, and b) the shop's heated or cooled air is retained.

Our dust-collection system features metal ducting. We chose metal because unlike PVC pipe, it doesn't require a ground wire to prevent a buildup of static charges. We ran the ducting through the accessible attic space to cut down on the amount of exposed ducting.

Note: *Metal ducting costs considerably more than PVC pipe, which in most home shops works as well.*

Dust collection in the Idea Shop™ didn't stop there. A mobile air-filtration cabinet—also an outfeed table—removes dust, too. You'll find plans for this project on page 56.

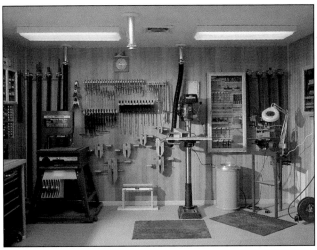

Tired of searching for clamps? In the Idea Shop™, we keep a full line at the ready on one wall, with each type having a specialized holder. Better still, they're only a few steps from the assembly workbench (removed from this photo but seen on *page 36*) where needed most.

The lathe parallels an end wall of the shop. Its mobile base allows you to swing it out for special turning tasks. Note the portable dust pickup behind the lathe and the turning-tool storage nearby.

In the finishing area, a fold-down platform with turntable supports small projects when spraying or brushing.

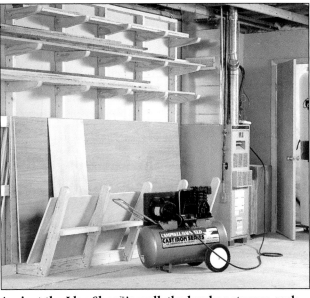

Against the Idea Shop™'s wall, the lumber-storage rack holds 12' boards and full sheets of plywood.

Dealing with fumes, flammables, fire, and theft

At the spray-finishing workstation, shown *above*, a filter-shielded, explosion-proof exhaust fan mounted in the wall (above the chair) removes toxic fumes through a 16x16" vent. The finishing area becomes self-contained with a wrap-around vinyl curtain which protects the rest of the shop from overspray by spray cans or a conventional spray gun.

In the same area, you'll find two storage cabinets—one OSHA-approved metal unit with double-walled protection for storing flammable liquids, and a second wall-mounted cabinet for painting equipment. Along the adjacent wall there's a red-lidded can for the safe disposal of oily rags and other finish waste.

By each shop door, we wall-mounted an ABC-rated fire extinguisher. And to detect a fire, should one occur, we had two 130° heat sensors installed in the shop's ceiling and connected to our shop security system and alarm.

UNIVERSAL WALL-CABINET SYSTEM

When we decided to build the Idea Shop™, we wanted every component to be fresh, new, and above all practical. With that in mind, I put my engineering background to work and designed a wall-cabinet system that works great for organizing hand tools, safety equipment, power-tool accessories, and much more. The cabinets go together quickly, they won't cost you an arm and a leg, and the acrylic inserts in the doors allow you to spot your well-organized tools in a jiffy and keep dust away from them, too.

On the following pages, we'll show you how to build a 2×4' cabinet. (For cabinets with different dimensions, see the sizing guidelines *opposite*.) Starting on *page 12*, we'll explain the method Jim Boelling, our Project Builder, used to design the tool holders in our cabinets. Turn to *page 14* for plans to build the Forstner bit holders.

—*Marlen Kemmet
How-to Editor*

Start with the back and the mounting strips

1. From ½" plywood, cut the back (A) to the size listed in the Bill of Materials.

2. Using the drawing *opposite, top* bevel-rip the 29 mounting strips (B) to size from ½"-thick stock. Crosscut the strips to length.

3. Mark the screw-hole centerpoints where dimensioned on the Exploded View drawing, and then drill and countersink a trio of shank holes in each strip.

4. To ensure consistent spacing between the strips and smooth-sliding components, build a spacing jig like that shown *opposite*.

How to size cabinets to suit your needs

The cabinet we show on the opposite pages measures 2x4'. But we've built various-sized cabinets for such things as our measuring and marking tools, lathe tools, air-powered tools, and hand planes, to name a few. To help size your custom cabinets, follow these planning guidelines:

•Gather together the tools or other items you want to store in a special purpose cabinet. The lay out the items on a large piece of plywood. This will give you a rough idea of how large to make the cabinet's back.

•If making your cabinet shorter or longer, do so in 1½" increments to allow for each mounting strip and a ¼" gap added or subtracted.

•If you widen a cabinet and the door becomes wider than it is tall, we recommend using two doors.

•Finally, make the depth of the cabinet equal to the width of the widest tool to be stored in the cabinet plus 1½".

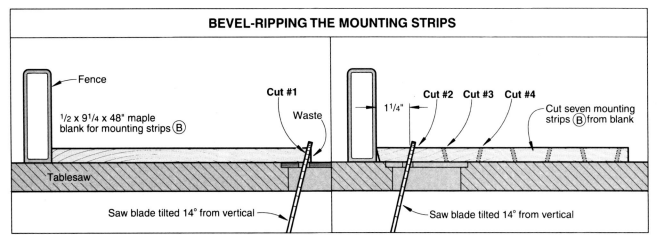

BEVEL-RIPPING THE MOUNTING STRIPS

Fence

½ x 9¼ x 48" maple blank for mounting strips Ⓑ

Tablesaw

Cut #1

Waste

Saw blade tilted 14° from vertical

1¼"

Cut #2 Cut #3 Cut #4

Cut seven mounting strips Ⓑ from blank

Saw blade tilted 14° from vertical

5. Clamp the back (A) to your workbench. Cut a piece of scrap measuring 2¼x22". With the top edges flush, clamp the scrap piece to the top of the back where shown in the photo *far right.*

6. Starting flush with the bottom edge of the scrap strip (2¼" from the top edge of the back), glue and screw the first mounting strip (B) to the back where shown in the photo. See the Mounting detail accompanying the Exploded View drawing for reference. Check that the ends of the mounting strip are flush with the outside edges of the back. Use only a small amount of glue to avoid squeeze-out. Immediately wipe off excess glue with a damp cloth.

Caution: Glue left between the mounting strips can prevent the tool holders from sliding easily in the dovetail grooves later.

7. To ensure consistent gaps between the mounting strips, use the spacing jig as shown *above right.* Working from the top down, glue and screw all the mounting strips to the back.

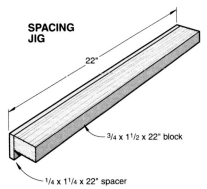

SPACING JIG

22"

¾ x 1½ x 22" block

¼ x 1¼ x 22" spacer

Now, construct the basic cabinet assembly

1. Cut the cabinet sides (C) and top and bottom (D) to the sizes listed in the Bill of Materials from ¾" birch plywood.

2. Cut a ¾" rabbet ½" deep across both ends of each side piece. Glue and clamp the pieces (C, D). Check for square, and wipe off excess glue. So the cabinet will easily fit onto the back (A) later, the opening is ⅟₁₆" larger in length and width than the back.

3. Cut the hanger strip (E) to size. For mounting the strip to the

Glue and screw the maple mounting strips to the plywood back, using the spacing jig for consistent gaps.

back later, mark the locations, and drill and countersink a pair of mounting holes through the front face of E where shown on the Exploded View drawing.

4. Glue and clamp the hanger strip to the bottom of the cabinet top (D), ½" in from the back edge. See the Mounting detail accompanying the Exploded View drawing for reference. Drill three mounting holes through the cabinet *continued*

UNIVERSAL WALL-CABINET SYSTEM
continued

top, centered into the top edge of the hanger strip (E). Drive a #8x1¼" wood screw through each hole just drilled.

5. Rip and miter-cut the face-frame strips (F, G) to size. Glue and clamp them to the front of the cabinet. Sand the strips flush with the cabinet frame.

6. Rout a ⅜" round-over along the outside front edge of the cabinet assembly (parts F and G).

7. Cut the door stops (H, I) to size.

8. For mounting the magnetic catches later, drill a pair of ¹¹⁄₃₂" holes ⅝" deep in one door stop (H) where shown on the Exploded View and Catch drawings. Hold off installing the door stops until final assembly.

For an open and shut case, add the door

1. Cut the maple door rails (J) and stiles (K) to size.

2. Cut 1½"-long half-lap joints on the ends of each rail and stile.

3. Glue and clamp the door frame members together, checking for square and making sure the frame clamps flat. Later, remove the clamps and sand the door smooth.

4. Rout a ¼" rabbet ⅜" deep along the back inside edge of the door frame for the acrylic panel and stops. Using a chisel, square the curved corners left by the router.

5. Fit your router with a ⅜" round-over bit, and rout along the front inside edge of the door frame. See the Section View detail accompanying the Door drawing for reference.

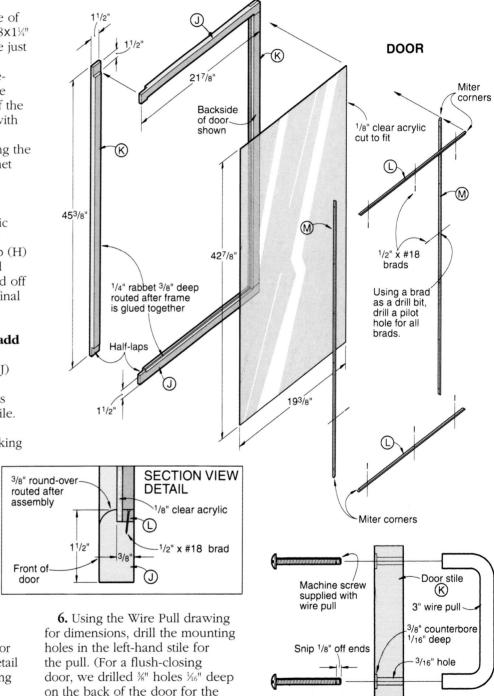

DOOR

SECTION VIEW DETAIL

WIRE PULL

6. Using the Wire Pull drawing for dimensions, drill the mounting holes in the left-hand stile for the pull. (For a flush-closing door, we drilled ⅜" holes ¹⁄₁₆" deep on the back of the door for the screw heads. Then, we used a

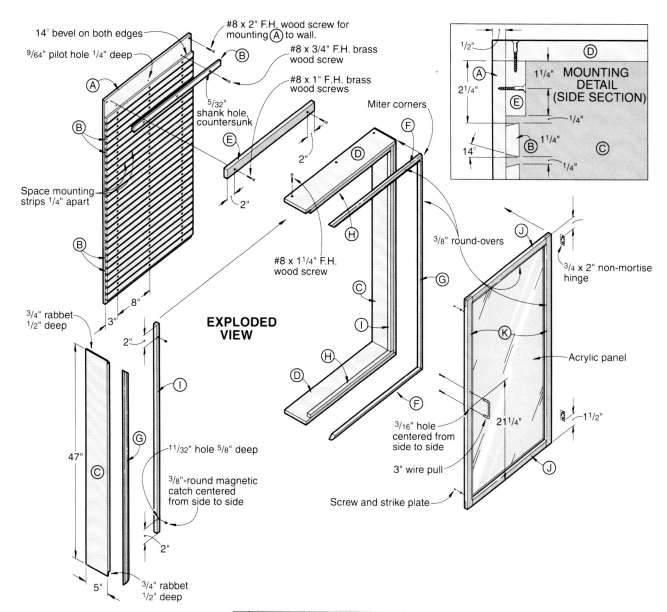

14° bevel on both edges

⁹⁄₆₄" pilot hole ¼" deep

Ⓐ

Ⓑ

Ⓑ

#8 x 2" F.H. wood screw for mounting Ⓐ to wall.

#8 x ¾" F.H. brass wood screw

Ⓑ

#8 x 1" F.H. brass wood screws

⁵⁄₃₂" shank hole, countersunk

Ⓔ

2"

2"

2"

Miter corners

Ⓕ

Ⓓ

Ⓗ

Space mounting strips ¼" apart

#8 x 1¼" F.H. wood screw

Ⓒ

Ⓘ

Ⓗ

Ⓓ

Ⓕ

Ⓖ

Ⓙ

³⁄₈" round-overs

³⁄₄ x 2" non-mortise hinge

Ⓚ

Acrylic panel

EXPLODED VIEW

8"

³⁄₄" rabbet ½" deep

3"

2"

21¼"

1½"

³⁄₁₆" hole centered from side to side

3" wire pull

Ⓙ

Screw and strike plate

Ⓘ

47"

Ⓒ

Ⓖ

¹¹⁄₃₂" hole ⁵⁄₈" deep

³⁄₈"-round magnetic catch centered from side to side

2"

5"

³⁄₄" rabbet ½" deep

MOUNTING DETAIL (SIDE SECTION)

½"

Ⓐ

2¼"

Ⓔ

1¼"

Ⓓ

¼"

Ⓑ

1¼"

Ⓒ

14°

¼"

combination bolt cutter/wire stripper to snip ⅛" off the end of each screw so the wire pull would draw tight to the door front.) See the Buying Guide for our hardware source.

7. Drill the pilot holes, and fasten a pair of no-mortise hinges to the right-hand door stile. Center the door top to bottom in the opening, and mark the mating hinge locations on the cabinet side. Drill mounting holes, and attach the hinges and door to the cabinet.

continued

Bill of Materials										
Parts	**Finished Size**			**Mat.**	**Qty.**	**Parts**	**Finished Size**			**Mat.**	**Qty.**
	T	**W**	**L**				**T**	**W**	**L**		
BACK AND STRIPS						**DOOR**					
A back	½"	22"	45½"	BP	1	I door stops	¾"	¾"	44"	M	2
B mounting						J rails	¾"	1½"	21⅞"	M	2
strips	½"	1¼"	22"	M	29	K stiles	¾"	1½"	45⅜"	M	2
CABINET FRAME						L stops	¼"	¼"	19⅜"	M	2
C sides	¾"	5"	47"	BP	2	M stops	¼"	¼"	42⅞"	M	2
D top/bottom	¾"	5"	23"	BP	2	**Material Key:** BP—birch plywood, M—maple					
E hanger						**Supplies:** #8X1¼" flathead wood screws,					
strip	¾"	2"	22"	M	1	#8X2" flathead wood screws, #8X1" flathead					
F face strips	¾"	¾"	23½"	M	2	brass wood screws, #8X¾" flathead brass wood					
G face strips	¾"	¾"	47"	M	2	screws, ⅛" clear acrylic, #18X½" brads, paint,					
H door stops	¾"	¾"	22"	M	2	clear finish.					

UNIVERSAL WALL-CABINET SYSTEM
continued

8. Cut the acrylic-panel stops (L, M) to size. Snip the head off a #18X½" brad, chuck the headless brad into your portable drill, and drill pilot holes through the stops. Do not install the acrylic yet.

Complete the assembly, add the finish, and hang

1. Insert a pair of magnetic catches into the holes in the left-hand door stop.

2. Fasten the door stops (H, I) to the cabinet so when swung shut, the front of the door is flush with the front of the cabinet.

3. Close the door tightly against the catches to mark their mating position on the back edge of the door stile (K). Next, using a brad-point bit, drill a ½" hole ¹⁄₁₆" in the door stile where indented for each strike plate. Using the centered depression left by the bradpoint bit when drilling the ½" hole, drill a ³⁄₃₂" pilot hole ⅜" deep centered inside the ½"-diameter counterbore. Screw the strike plates in place.

4. Remove the hardware (except for the magnetic catches) from the cabinet and door. Finish-sand the cabinet assembly, back, door, and acrylic panel stops.

5. Mask the surrounding areas and catches, and apply a clear finish to the face strips, door stops, mounting strips, and door.

6. Mask the maple face strips (F, G), and then paint the cabinet.

7. Measure the openings, and have an acrylic panel cut to fit. Secure the panel with the stops (L, M).

8. Reattach the wire pull and hinges to the door. Reattach the door to the cabinet.

9. To mount the back (A) to the wall, locate the stud(s), and position the back. Drill mounting

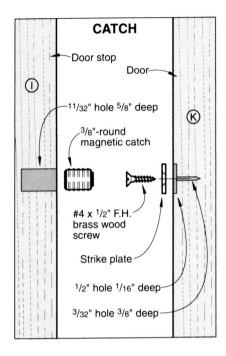

CATCH

Door stop

Door

¹¹⁄₃₂" hole ⅝" deep

³⁄₈"-round magnetic catch

#4 x ¹⁄₂" F.H. brass wood screw

Strike plate

¹⁄₂" hole ¹⁄₁₆" deep

³⁄₃₂" hole ³⁄₈" deep

holes through the top and bottom of the back, centered over the stud(s). Check for plumb and level, and secure the back to the wall. Fit the cabinet assembly onto the back, and secure it to the back by driving a set of screws through the hanger strip (E) and into the back. After you've built your organizers, remove the cabinet from the back, slide the organizers in place, and reattach the cabinet to the back. To adjust the organizers, simply remove the three screws from the top of the cabinet top (D), and remove the cabinet from the backboard assembly (A, B, E).

Buying Guide

• **Hardware.** 3" polished-brass wire pull, two magnetic catches with strike plates, and two ¾x2" no-mortise hinges. Kit No. 71159 (enough for one cabinet). Kit No. 71167, for two kits, and Kit No. 71168 for five kits. For current

prices, contact Klockit, P.O. Box 636, Lake Geneva, WI 53147, or call 800-556-2548 to order.

Customized Tool Holders

Now that you've built a cabinet or two using our Idea Shop™ wall-cabinet design, it's time to add some customized holders. But before you begin, familiarize yourself with a holder's parts.

Anatomy of a tool holder

As shown *opposite, top left,* we call the horizontal part that supports the tool the **shelf.** For heavier items, the shelf fits into a groove in the support. The **dovetail strip** attaches to the back of a shelf or support and slides between the mounting strips. The **banding strips** protect tools from falling off the front or ends of the shelf.

Make your holders to fit

To make the shelf, start by laying the item you want to store on a piece of stock. (We used ½"- and ¾"-thick maple for most shelves.) If the bottom of the tool is square or rectangular, cut the shelf about ⅛" oversize. Or, for screwdrivers, router bits, and other shanked items, cut the shelf to size, and drill holes for the tool shanks where shown on the Screwdriver Holder drawing. The distance between holes depends on the items you intend to store.

Next, add the banding strips

These should extend high enough above the shelf (usually about ¼" to keep the tool from being bumped off. We used banded shelves for the planes, sharpening stones, drill bit index boxes, and other flat-bottomed

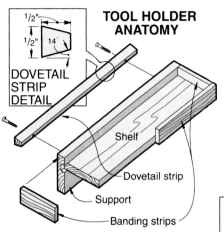

TOOL HOLDER ANATOMY

1/2"
1/2" 14

DOVETAIL STRIP DETAIL

Shelf

Dovetail strip

Support

Banding strips

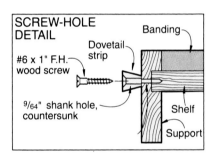

SCREW-HOLE DETAIL

Banding

Dovetail strip

#6 x 1" F.H. wood screw

9/64" shank hole, countersunk

Shelf

Support

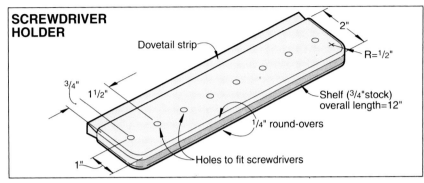

SCREWDRIVER HOLDER

Dovetail strip

2"

R=1/2"

3/4"

1 1/2"

Shelf (3/4"stock) overall length=12"

1/4" round-overs

1"

Holes to fit screwdrivers

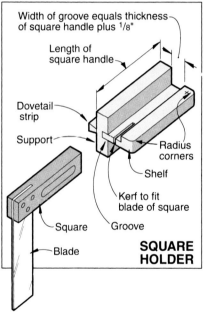

Width of groove equals thickness of square handle plus 1/8"

Length of square handle

Dovetail strip

Support

Radius corners

Shelf

Kerf to fit blade of square

Square

Groove

Blade

SQUARE HOLDER

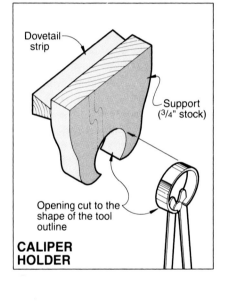

Dovetail strip

Support (3/4" stock)

Opening cut to the shape of the tool outline

CALIPER HOLDER

items. If the tool's outline is irregular like that of the caliper holder on the opposite page, mark a portion of the tool's outline on 3/4" stock. Then, cut the outline to shape.

Now, add the dovetail strips

Bevel-rip long lengths of dovetail-strip stock at 14°. See the Dovetail Strip detail accompanying the Tool Holder Anatomy drawing *top left* for reference. Crosscut the dovetail strips to length. Drill and countersink mounting holes in the back edge of the strip. Glue and screw the dovetail strip to the back edge of the shelf, support, or holder.

Slide the dovetail strip of the holder between the mounting strips in the cabinet back. If the dovetail strip fits too tightly between the mounting strips, sand it slightly for a smooth sliding action. Remove and finish holders.

Once dry, slide your holders between the mounting strips in the cabinet back (attached to the wall at this point). Arrange the holders as needed, secure the cabinet back to the wall. You're ready to add your tools and accessories.

FORSTNER BIT HOLDERS FOR THE DRILL-PRESS CABINET

Here's a handy pair of holders to fit inside our universal wall-cabinet system shown *below.* To make each holder, bevel-rip the dovetail strips (A, D) to size. Next, cut the top and bottom shelf pieces (B, C and E, F) to size and shape for each holder. Bore the holes in each top piece (B and E). Laminate the mating pieces pieces together for each holder.

Cut the slots for the bit shank with a bandsaw or scrollsaw. Drill the mounting holes through the dovetail strips, and glue and screw them to the back edge of each laminated shelf.

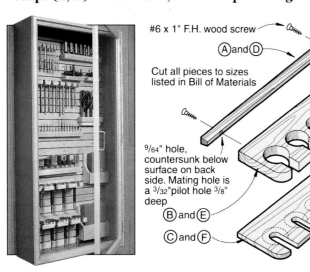

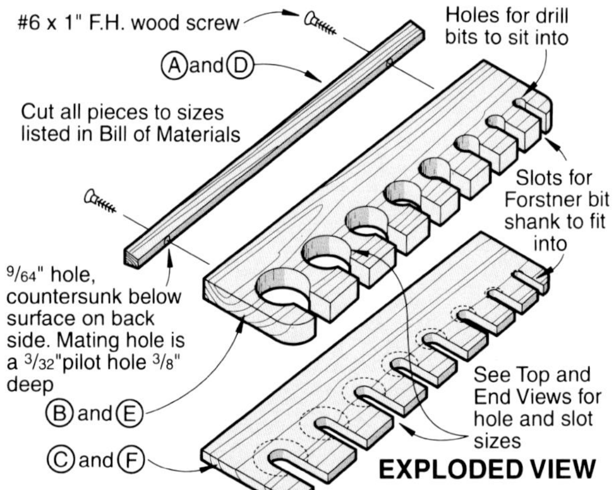

#6 x 1" F.H. wood screw

Ⓐ and Ⓓ

Cut all pieces to sizes listed in Bill of Materials

Holes for drill bits to sit into

Slots for Forstner bit shank to fit into

9/64" hole, countersunk below surface on back side. Mating hole is a 3/32" pilot hole 3/8" deep

Ⓑ and Ⓔ

Ⓒ and Ⓕ

See Top and End Views for hole and slot sizes

EXPLODED VIEW

Bill of Materials

Part	Finished Size			Mat.	Qty.
	T	W	L		
A	½"	½"	8¾"	M	1
B	½"	2½"	8¾"	M	1
C	¼"	2½"	8¾"	M	1
D	½"	½"	14"	M	1
E	½"	3"	14"	M	1
F	¼"	3"	14"	M	1

Material Key: M—maple
Supplies: #6X¾" F.H. wood screws, finish.

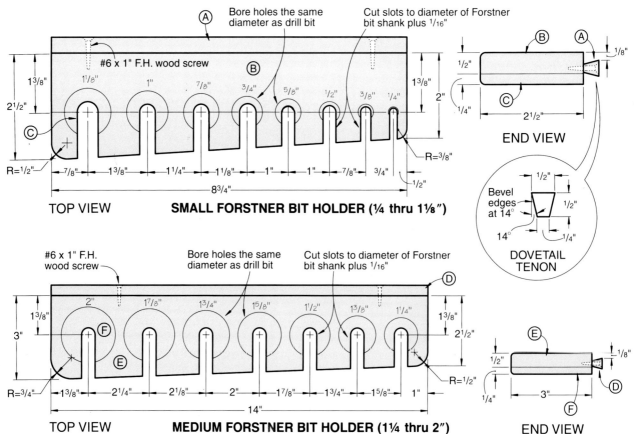

Ⓐ

Bore holes the same diameter as drill bit

Cut slots to diameter of Forstner bit shank plus 1/16"

#6 x 1" F.H. wood screw

Ⓑ

1⅛" 1" 7/8" 3/4" 5/8" ½" 3/8" ¼"

1⅜" 2½" Ⓒ R=½"

7/8" 1⅜" 1¼" 1⅛" 1" 1" 7/8" 3/4"

8¾"

R=3/8" ½" 1⅜" 2"

TOP VIEW   **SMALL FORSTNER BIT HOLDER (¼ thru 1⅛")**

Ⓑ Ⓐ 1/8"
½" ½" Ⓒ ¼" 2½"

END VIEW

Bevel edges at 14° 14° ½" ½" ¼"

DOVETAIL TENON

#6 x 1" F.H. wood screw

Bore holes the same diameter as drill bit

Cut slots to diameter of Forstner bit shank plus 1/16"

Ⓓ

2" 1⅞" 1¾" 1⅝" 1½" 1⅜" 1¼"

Ⓕ Ⓔ

1⅜" 3" 1⅜" 2½"

R=3/4" 1⅜" 2¼" 2⅛" 2" 1⅞" 1¾" 1⅝" 1" R=½"

14"

TOP VIEW   **MEDIUM FORSTNER BIT HOLDER (1¼ thru 2")**

Ⓔ 1/8"
½" 3" Ⓓ
¼" Ⓕ

END VIEW

SANDING-SUPPLY ORGANIZER

L ooking for that single location where you can store all
of your sanding supplies? This
WOOD ® magazine original,
featuring a half-dozen easy-to-
build projects, may be just the
ticket. It includes holders for
belts, sanding discs and accessories, stick sanders and strips,
hand sanders, and rolls of
adhesive-backed sandpaper.

Ordering Information

For our center, we used mostly
3M products, which you can find at
home centers, hardware stores,
contractors supply outlets, and
through woodworking mail-order
catalogs. Or, order them from:

    Puckett Electric
    841 11th Street
    Des Moines, IA 50309
    Call 800-544-4189 or
    515-244-4189 to order.

1. Sanding-stick and sandpaper-strip organizer

When that hand-crafted project
requires precision
sanding, this trio
of sanding sticks
and adhesive-
backed sandpaper
strips performs
admirably. Build
the solid-maple
organizer to
divide the coarse-,
medium-, and
fine-grit sand-
paper strips,
using the drawing
and Bill of Materials on *page
16*. Then, refer to the full-sized
pattern to make the contour-
handled sticks.

continued

Guide to our six great organizers
1. Sanding-stick and
sandpaper-strip organizer
2. 5" sanding-disc holder
3. Hand-sander rack and tote
4. Disc-sander center
5. Roll-sandpaper dispenser
6. Belt-sander belt divider

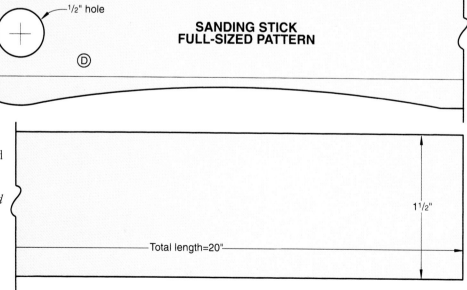

½" hole

**SANDING STICK
FULL-SIZED PATTERN**

D

1½"

Total length=20"

SANDING-SUPPLY ORGANIZER

continued

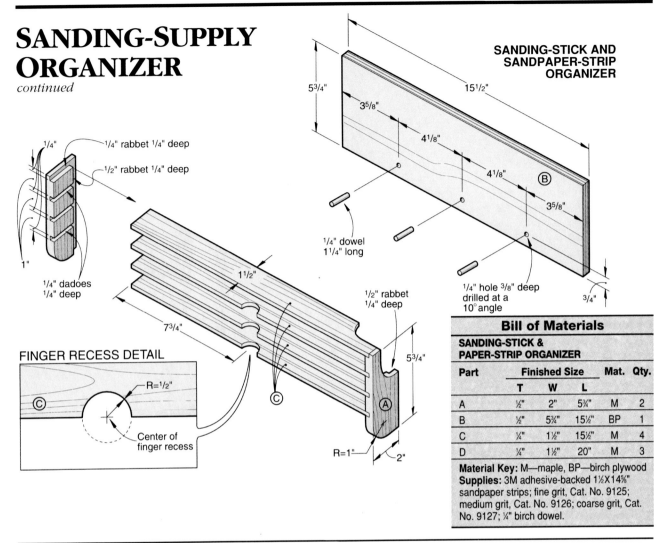

SANDING-STICK AND SANDPAPER-STRIP ORGANIZER

¼"

¼" rabbet ¼" deep

½" rabbet ¼" deep

1"

¼" dadoes ¼" deep

1½"

7¾"

½" rabbet ¼" deep

5¾"

R=1"

2"

5¾"

15½"

3⁵⁄₈"

4⅛"

4⅛"

3⁵⁄₈"

¼" dowel 1¼" long

¼" hole ⅜" deep drilled at a 10° angle

¾"

Ⓐ Ⓑ Ⓒ

FINGER RECESS DETAIL

Ⓒ

R=½"

Center of finger recess

Bill of Materials				
SANDING-STICK & PAPER-STRIP ORGANIZER				
Part	**Finished Size**		Mat.	Qty.
	T	W	L	
A	½"	2"	5¾"	M	2
B	½"	5¾"	15½"	BP	1
C	¼"	1½"	15½"	M	4
D	¼"	1½"	20"	M	3

Material Key: M—maple, BP—birch plywood
Supplies: 3M adhesive-backed 1½X14⅝" sandpaper strips; fine grit, Cat. No. 9125; medium grit, Cat. No. 9126; coarse grit, Cat. No. 9127; ¼" birch dowel.

Bill of Materials				
5" SANDING-DISC HOLDER				
Part	**Finished Size**		Mat.	Qty.
	T	W	L	
A	½"	5¼"	7"	M	2
B	½"	5¼"	5¾"	M	2
C	¼"	5¾"	6½"	BP	1
D	¼"	5"	5¾"	M	4

Material Key: M—maple, BP—birch plywood
Supplies: 3M adhesive-backed 5" discs; fine grit, Cat. No. 9170; medium grit, Cat. No. 9171; coarse grit, Cat. No. 9172.

2. 5" Sanding-disc holder

Adhered to a shanked disc pad and powered by your portable drill, a sanding disc allows you to sand contours with minimum effort. The discs press on and peel off, making for quick changes to the next grit. For larger-sized discs, simply increase the depth and width of the holder.

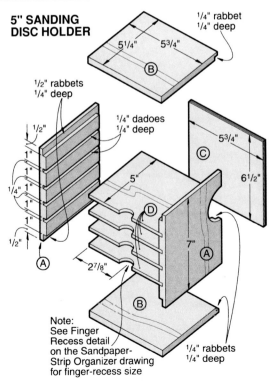

5" SANDING DISC HOLDER

¼" rabbet ¼" deep

5¼" 5¾"

Ⓑ

½" rabbets ¼" deep

½"

1"

1"

¼"

1"

½"

Ⓐ

¼" dadoes ¼" deep

5¾"

Ⓒ

6½"

5"

Ⓓ

7"

Ⓐ

2⅞"

Ⓑ

Note: See Finger Recess detail on the Sandpaper-Strip Organizer drawing for finger-recess size

¼" rabbets ¼" deep

3. Hand-sander tote and rack

Carry a quartet of hand sanders—each having a different grit—to your workbench with this handy tote. When you're done, just return the tote to the rack. You'll also find room for rolls of adhesive-backed sandpaper behind the hand sanders in the tote.

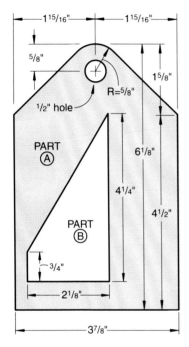

PARTS VIEWS

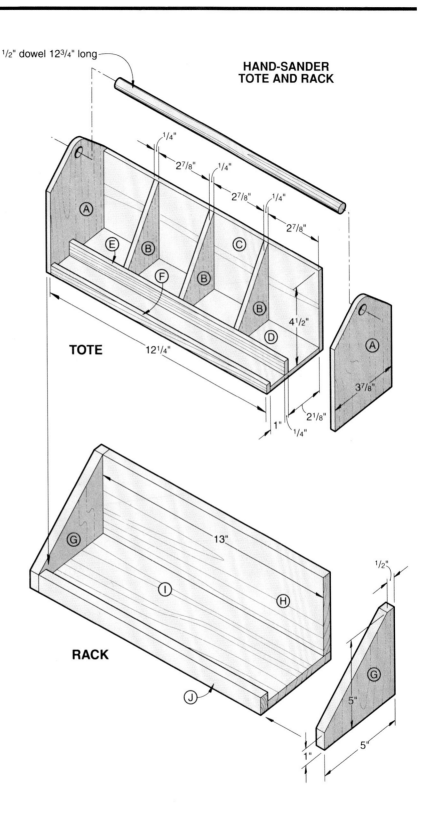

HAND-SANDER TOTE AND RACK

TOTE

RACK

Bill of Materials				
HAND-SANDER TOTE AND RACK				
Part	**Finished Size**		**Mat.**	**Qty.**
	T	**W**	**L**		
TOTE					
A	¼"	3⅞"	6⅛"	M	2
B	¼"	2⅛"	4¼"	M	3
C	¼"	4½"	12¼"	M	1
D	¼"	3⅜"	12¼"	M	1
E	¼"	¾"	12¼"	M	1
F	¼"	½"	12¼"	M	1
TOTE RACK					
G	½"	5"	5"	M	2
H	½"	4½"	13"	M	1
I	½"	4½"	13"	M	1
J	½"	1"	13"	M	1

Material Key: M—maple
Supplies: 3M Hand Ease sander, Cat. No. 45204. Sandpaper roll refills; very fine, 2½X90", Cat. No. 10124; fine, 2½X80", Cat. No. 10125; medium, 2½ X55", Cat. No. 10126.

continued

SANDING-SUPPLY ORGANIZER
continued

Bill of Materials				
DISC-SANDER CENTER				
Part	Finished Size		Mat.	Qty.
	T	W	L	
A	½"	3½"	15½"	M	2
B	½"	3½"	7¼"	M	2
C	½"	3¼"	7¼"	M	4
D	¼"	3¼"	2½"	M	4
E	¼"	3¼"	1¾"	M	1
F	¼"	3¼"	3½"	M	4
G	¼"	7¼"	15"	BP	1

Material Key: M—maple, BP—birch plywood
Supplies: disc-sanding kits available through most woodworking mail-order suppliers.

4. Disc-sander center

You can't beat small-diameter disc sanders for sanding the contours of shapely projects and the inside and outside of turned bowls. Here's a slick way to get your sanding-adhesive drill attachments and various discs in order and divided by grit.

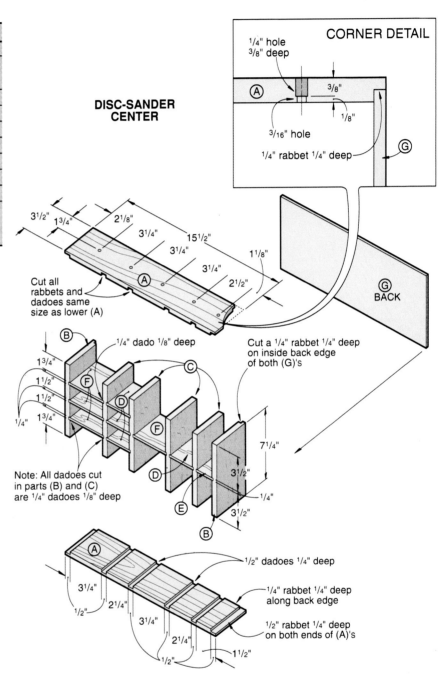

5. Roll-sandpaper dispenser

This handy dispenser lets you store up to four 4½"-wide rolls of sandpaper. It loads from the bottom, and is dimensioned to let you tear off 4" pieces, perfect for the palm sander.

To remove a needed piece, pull the end of the sandpaper roll flush with the front top edge of Part C.

Fold a crease in the sandpaper along the back edge of Part C (4" from the front). Pull the paper out until the crease aligns with the front edge of C. Adhere the paper back to Part C so the crease is flush with the front edge. Just pull down on the paper to tear off a 4"-long piece.

Bill of Materials
ROLL-SANDPAPER DISPENSER

Part	Finished Size			Mat.	Qty.
	T	W	L		
A	½"	3½"	9"	M	2
B	½"	4½"	21"	M	1
C	½"	4"	20"	M	1
D	½"	3"	20"	M	1
E	⅛"	3"	20½"	M	1
F	½"	3" diam.		M	3
G	½"	3½"	20"	M	1
H	¼"	1⅜"	2¼"	M	1

Material Key: M—maple
Supplies: 3M adhesive-backed sandpaper rolls 4½"-wide by 10 yards long, 80-grit, Cat. No. 00395; 100-grit, 00396; 120-grit, 00397; 220-grit, 00399; #8X⅝" flathead wood screws, #17X¾" brads.

ROLL-SANDPAPER DISPENSER

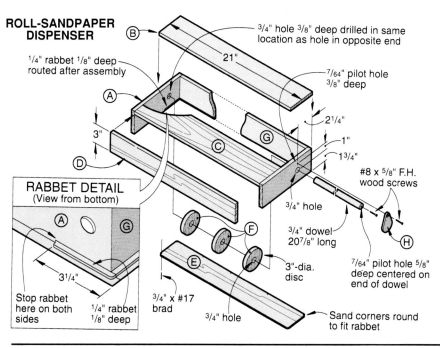

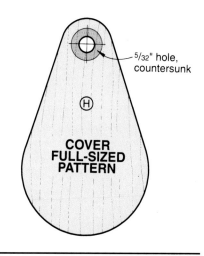

6. Belt-sander divider

We sized our divider for holding 3"-wide sanding belts. For wider belts, just increase the width of pieces B and C.

Bill of Materials
BELT-SANDER BELT DIVIDER

Part	Finished Size			Mat.	Qty.
	T	W	L		
A	½"	10"	20"	M	2
B	½"	3¾"	10"	M	2
C	½"	3¾"	9¾"	M	5
D	¼"	3¾"	19½"	BP	1

Material Key: M—maple, BP—birch plywood

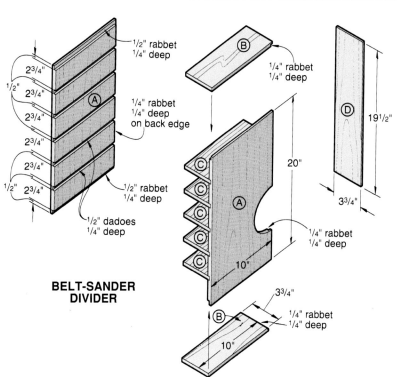

BELT-SANDER DIVIDER

19

CLAMP-STORAGE EXTRAVAGANZA

Guide to our five great holders
1. Spring-clamp holder
2. Sliding-head and quick-grip clamp rack
3. Locking C-clamp support
4. C-clamp rack
5. Handscrew clamp organizer

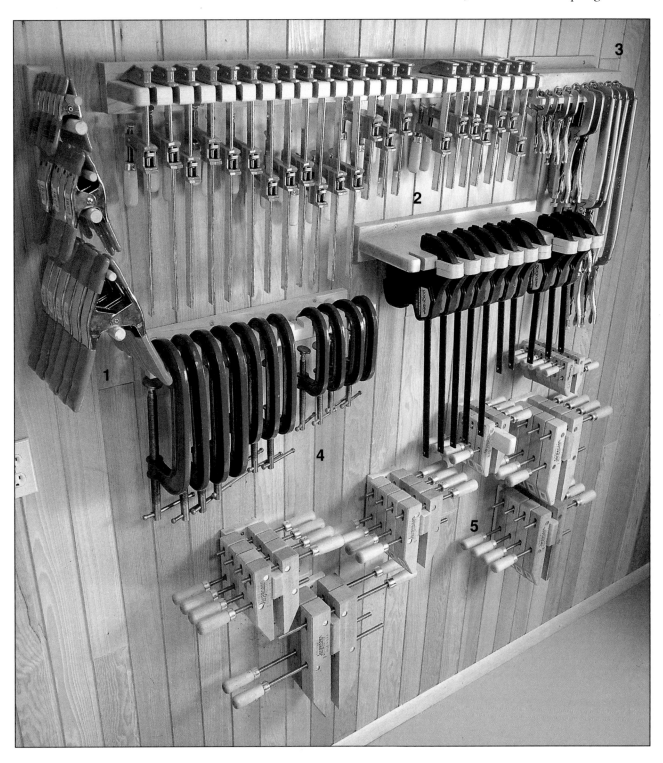

Solve your clamp-storage problem once and for all with this fine selection of wall-hung helpers proven effective in our Idea Shop.™ Not only do they keep all your clamps at arm's reach, they also look darn good doing it.

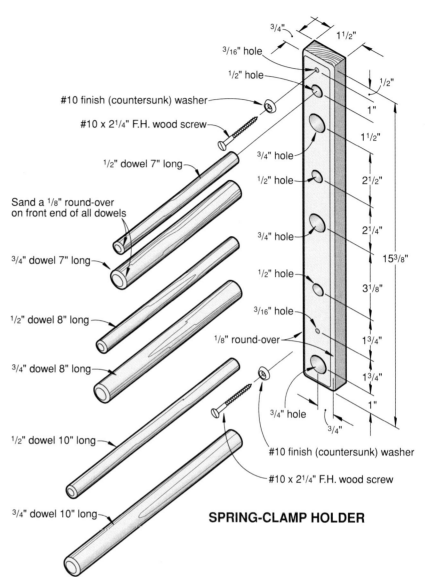

Spring-clamp holder labels:
- 3/4"
- 1 1/2"
- 3/16" hole
- 1/2" hole
- #10 finish (countersunk) washer
- #10 x 2 1/4" F.H. wood screw
- 1/2" dowel 7" long
- Sand a 1/8" round-over on front end of all dowels
- 3/4" dowel 7" long
- 3/4" hole
- 1/2" hole
- 1/2" dowel 8" long
- 3/4" dowel 8" long
- 3/4" hole
- 1/2" hole
- 3/16" hole
- 1/8" round-over
- 1/2" dowel 10" long
- 3/4" dowel 10" long
- #10 finish (countersunk) washer
- #10 x 2 1/4" F.H. wood screw
- 3/4" hole
- 1/2"
- 1"
- 1 1/2"
- 2 1/2"
- 2 1/4"
- 3 1/8"
- 15 3/8"
- 1 3/4"
- 1 3/4"
- 1"
- 3/4"

SPRING-CLAMP HOLDER

1. Simple, sturdy, spring-clamp holder

A backboard with protruding dowels does the job for supporting 4", 6", and 9"-long spring clamps. If you've got a similar assortment of these clamps, the rack shown here should suffice, If you've got quite a collection, extend the board or make two or more holders as needed.

We don't recommend extending the dowels longer than dimensioned on the drawing *above right.* Extended too far, they can get bumped and broken.

2. A home for sliding-head and Quick-Grip clamps

The slots in this quick-and-easy holder allow you to store your sliding-head clamps in perfect order by simply resting the head on the horizontal support. Without the slots, you'd have to tighten the jaws to hold a clamp in place, and then loosen the jaws when you want to remove the clamp from the holder.

To make the slots, cut the horizontal support to shape, rout the edges and corners, and mark the notches 1⅝" on center. Mount a ⅜" dado blade to your tablesaw, and raise the blade 2" above the saw table. Mount a wood extension to your miter gauge, and make the cuts where marked. As shown in the opening photo, we built and placed three racks *continued*

CLAMP-STORAGE EXTRAVAGANZA
continued

end to end. You could also lengthen the two parts and cut the number of slots needed to match your supply of clamps.

For Quick-Grip clamps, we found that an extended version (2¾" more from front to back) of the rack used to support our sliding-head clamps works wonderfully. The front support with its numerous slots holds the clamps upright and keeps them from dinging the wall.

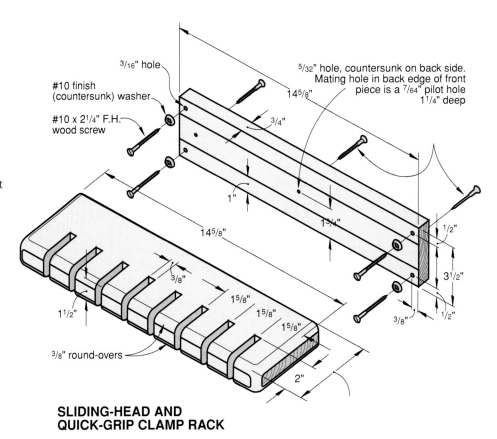

SLIDING-HEAD AND QUICK-GRIP CLAMP RACK

3. Nifty support for locking C-clamps

Projects often require clamping pressure applied several inches in from the outside edges for a good bond. When this happens, we turn to our locking C-clamps, the largest of which has a throat depth of over 15". To hang our collection of locking C-clamps, we found this screw-together support an organizer's dream.

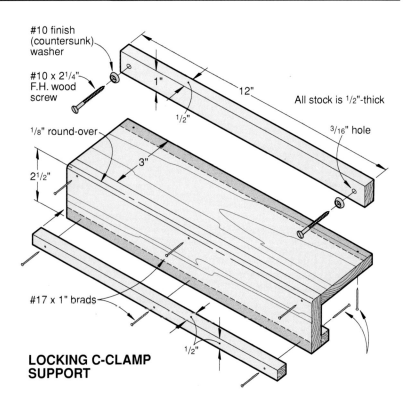

LOCKING C-CLAMP SUPPORT

4. All-in-a-row C-clamp rack

When the job calls for plenty of clamping pressure, no-nonsense C-clamps provide the answer. To hang and organize this type of clamp, build our four-piece wall-mounted hanger with its notched front support. The notches allow you to hang the clamps on the rack without having to tighten them.

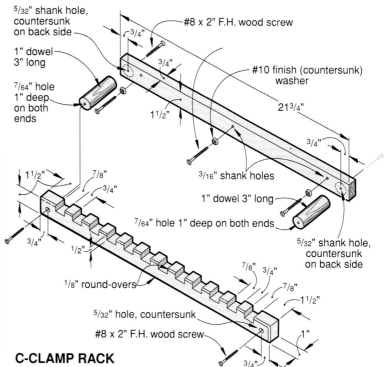

5/32" shank hole, countersunk on back side

#8 x 2" F.H. wood screw

1" dowel 3" long

3/4"

3/4"

#10 finish (countersunk) washer

7/64" hole 1" deep on both ends

1 1/2"

21 3/4"

3/4"

1 1/2"

7/8"

3/4"

3/16" shank holes

1" dowel 3" long

7/64" hole 1" deep on both ends

5/32" shank hole, countersunk on back side

3/4"

1/2"

1/8" round-overs

7/8"

3/4"

7/8"

1 1/2"

5/32" hole, countersunk

#8 x 2" F.H. wood screw

1"

3/4"

C-CLAMP RACK

5. Handscrew clamp hangout

If there was ever a simpler organizer for handscrew clamps, we haven't seen it. Just cut the support extension (A) to fit between the threaded rods of the clamp, chamfer the outside end of the support, and securely mount it to the backboard (B). We've found that about four clamps per support is a full load.

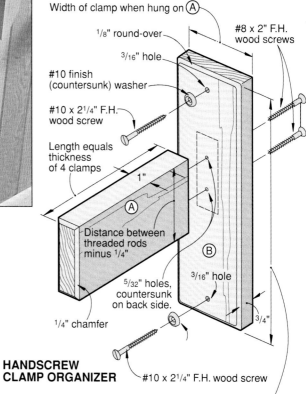

Width of clamp when hung on (A)

1/8" round-over

3/16" hole

#10 finish (countersunk) washer

#10 x 2 1/4" F.H. wood screw

#8 x 2" F.H. wood screws

Length equals thickness of 4 clamps

1"

(A)

Distance between threaded rods minus 1/4"

(B)

3/16" hole

5/32" holes, countersunk on back side.

1/4" chamfer

3/4"

HANDSCREW CLAMP ORGANIZER

#10 x 2 1/4" F.H. wood screw

LUMBER STORAGE RACK

Looking for versatility in a lumber storage rack? This one's got it! Our rack features adjustable supports that attach to vertical 2×4s for holding loads of boards. The unique sheet-goods bin lets you easily sort through heavy sheets and slide out the one you want. There's even between-the-studs storage for short stock and dowels.

Let's start with the wall framework

Note: We built our rack to fit against an existing drywalled wall. If you have an exposed stud wall and would like to use it, skip this section and build only the storage rack components covered in the later sections.

1. Measure the distance between your floor and ceiling. The overall height of the rack should be ¼" less than the measured distance.

2. From 2×4 stock, crosscut the top and bottom plates (A), uprights (B), and spacers (C) to length. Lay out the holes for the board supports on the uprights (B) where dimensioned on the Wall Framework drawing. Bore the ⁹⁄₁₆" holes where marked.

3. Position the pieces on the floor, and screw the framework together in the configuration shown on the Wall drawing. Square the uprights with the bottom plate.

Caution: Considering the amount of weight this unit can hold, you must securely anchor the framework to wall studs and ceiling joists. If the joists run perpendicular to the top plate, screw through the top plate and directly into them. If the joists are parallel to the top plate, install 2×4 blocking between the joists, and screw the top plate to the blocking.

4. With a helper, lift the wall framework into position. Shim the top plate against the ceiling, and firmly secure the top plate to the joists in your shop's ceiling (we used ¼" lag screws 3½" long). If you can hit wall studs, drill

continued

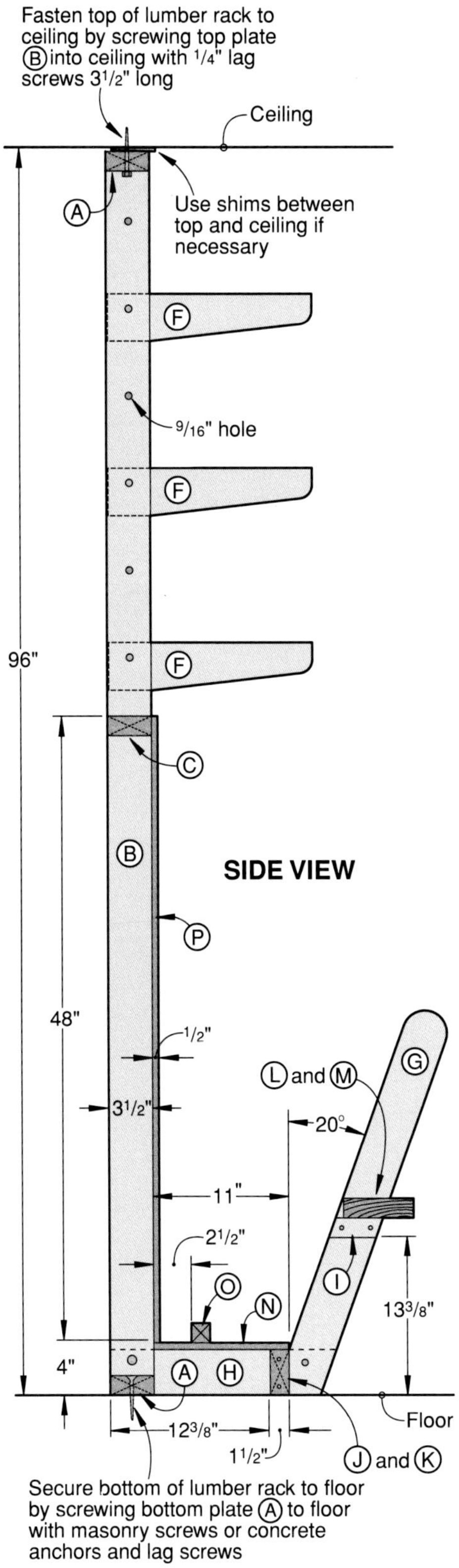

Fasten top of lumber rack to ceiling by screwing top plate Ⓑ into ceiling with 1/4" lag screws 3 1/2" long
Ceiling
Ⓐ
Use shims between top and ceiling if necessary
Ⓕ
9/16" hole
Ⓕ
96"
Ⓕ
Ⓒ
Ⓑ
SIDE VIEW
Ⓟ
48"
1/2"
3 1/2"
Ⓛ and Ⓜ
Ⓖ
20°
11"
2 1/2"
Ⓞ
Ⓝ
Ⓘ
13 3/8"
4"
Ⓐ Ⓗ
Floor
12 3/8"
1 1/2"
Ⓙ and Ⓚ
Secure bottom of lumber rack to floor by screwing bottom plate Ⓐ to floor with masonry screws or concrete anchors and lag screws

CUTTING DIAGRAM

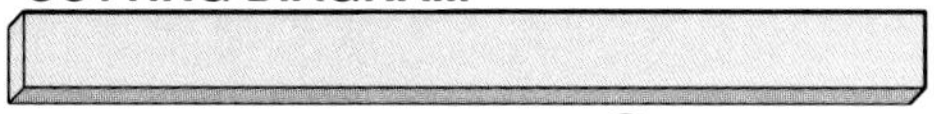

(2) 1 1/2 x 3 1/2" x 12' Fir (2x4's for Ⓐ)
(17) 1 1/2 x 3 1/2 x 96" Fir
(2x4's for Ⓑ,Ⓒ,Ⓔ,Ⓖ,Ⓗ,Ⓘ,Ⓙ,Ⓚ and Ⓞ)
(1) 1 1/2 x 5 1/2 x 96" Fir (2x6's for Ⓛ and Ⓜ)
(2) 1/2 x 48 x 96" Plywood
(for Ⓓ,Ⓕ,Ⓝ and Ⓟ)

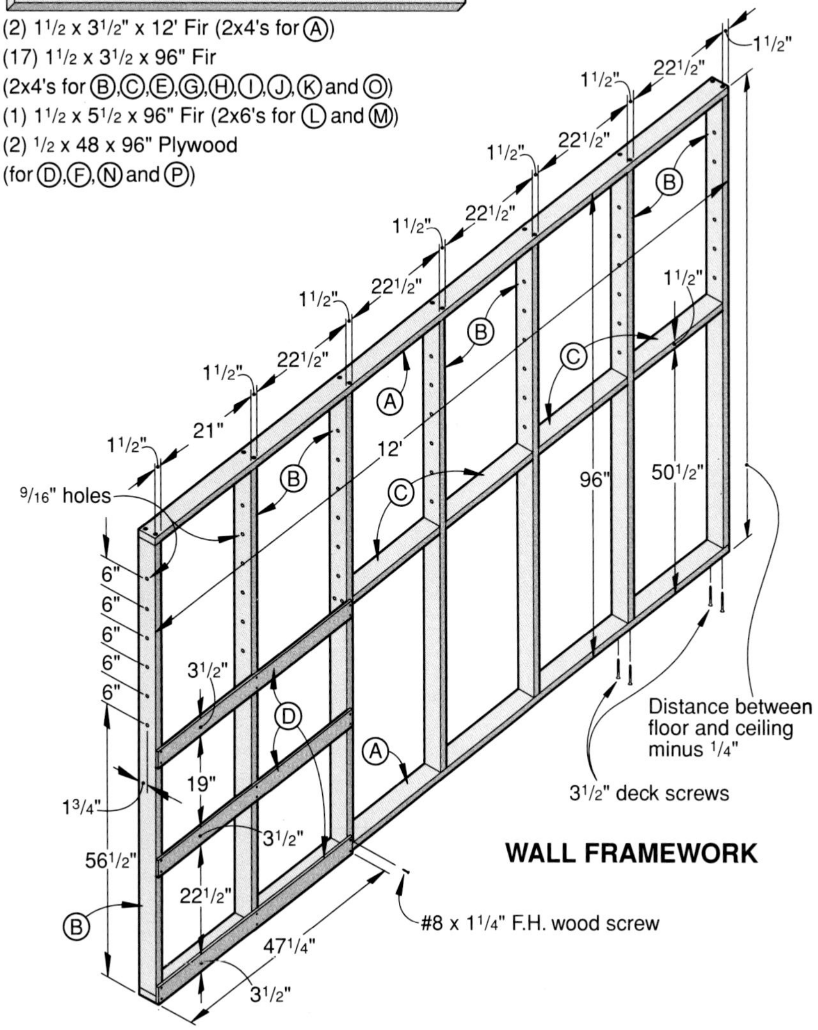

1 1/2"
22 1/2"
1 1/2"
Ⓑ
Ⓑ
1 1/2"
Ⓒ
21"
Ⓐ
12'
9/16" holes
Ⓑ
Ⓒ
96"
50 1/2"
6"
6"
6"
6"
6"
3 1/2"
Ⓓ
Ⓐ
19"
1 3/4"
3 1/2"
56 1/2"
22 1/2"
Ⓑ
47 1/4"
3 1/2"
#8 x 1 1/4" F.H. wood screw
Distance between floor and ceiling minus 1/4"
3 1/2" deck screws
WALL FRAMEWORK

Bill of Materials

Parts	Finished Size T	W	L	Mat.	Qty.
WALL FRAMEWORK					
A top & btm plates	1½"	3½"	12'	C	2
B* uprights	1½"	3½"	93"	C	7
C spacers	1½"	3½"	22½"	C	4
D stops	½"	3½"	47¼"	PLY	3
BOARD SUPPORTS					
E center	1½"	3½"	12"	C	21
F sides	½"	3½"	15½"	PLY	42
SHEET-GOODS BIN					
G angled supports	1½"	3½"	32"	C	5
H floor supports	1½"	3½"	18"	C	5
I cleats	¾"	1½"	4¼"	C	8
J spacers	1½"	3½"	22½"	C	3
K spacer	1½"	3½"	19½"	C	1
L steps	1½"	5½"	22½"	C	3
M step	1½"	5½"	19½"	C	1
N floor	½"	11"	94½"	PLY	1
O cleat	1½"	1½"	94½"	C	1
P back	½"	48"	96"	PLY	1

*Length will depend on distance from floor to ceiling at chosen rack location.

Material Key: C—choice (fir, pine, spruce), PLY—plywood.

Supplies: 3½" deck screws, #8X1¼" flathead wood screws, #8X1½" flathead wood screws, #8X2½" flat head wood screws, #8X3" flathead wood screws, ¼" lag screws 3½" long with flat washers, ½" carriage bolts 2" long with flat washers and nuts, ½" carriage bolts 3" long with flat washers and nuts, ½" carriage bolts 3½" long with flat washers and nuts, paraffin wax, masonry screws.

LUMBER STORAGE RACK
continued

2"-deep counterbored holes through the uprights (B) or spacers (C) and use 3"-long screws to further secure the framework.

5. Secure the bottom plate to your floor (we drilled holes in the concrete, and used plastic concrete anchors and lag screws; masonry screws also would work).

6. From ¾" plywood or 1×4s, cut the short-stock bin stops (D) to size, and screw them in place.

Now, let's build the board supports

1. Referring to the Board Support drawing, cut 21 center sections (E) and 42 plywood side pieces (F) to size.

2. Spread an even coat of glue on both faces of each center section (E), and clamp it between two of the side pieces (F), with the top edges and outside end flush.

3. After the glue dries, transfer the profile of one of the supports onto one of the laminations. Bandsaw the support to shape, and sand the cut edges smooth to remove the saw marks. Then, use this as a template to mark the profile onto the rest of the supports. Cut and sand them to shape.

The sheet-goods bin comes next

1. Using the Sheet-Goods Support drawing and accompanying details, cut the angled supports (G), floor supports (H), and cleats (I) to size. Cut 20° half-lap joints in the H and I pieces where shown on the drawing. Referring to the Cleat detail, miter the ends of the step cleats (I) at 20°.

2. Cut a 1½×3½" notch in the back of each floor support (H) where shown on the drawing.

3. Glue and clamp the supports together. After the glue dries, cut off the waste areas, where shown on the Hole detail.

4. Mark the centerpoints and drill a pair of ½" holes in each glued half lap and a single ½" hole above each

notch. To strengthen the joints, add a pair of carriage bolts with flat washers and nuts to each half-lap joint.

5. Drill the mounting holes, and glue and screw the stop cleats to the angled supports (G).

6. Clamp the support assemblies (G, H, I) to the uprights (B) where shown on the Sheet-Goods Bin Exploded View drawing and accompanying Support detail. Using the previously drilled holes above the notches in H as guides, drill the holes through the uprights. Install carriage bolts to secure the support assemblies to the 2×4 uprights.

7. From 2×4 and 2×6 stock, cut the floor spacers (J, K) and steps (L, M) to length. Drill mounting holes (some need to be angled), and glue and screw the pieces in place. Position each step (L, M), so the back edge won't protrude into

the plywood bin and possibly damage any stored sheet goods when pressed against the angled supports.

8. Cut the bin floor (N) and the floor cleat (O) to size. Position the pieces, drill mounting holes where shown on the Exploded View drawing, and attach them to the floor supports (H). To make the sheet goods slide in and out even easier, rub the bin with paraffin wax.

9. Lay out and drill pilot holes on the bin back (P), and attach with wood screws.

10. Using ½" carriage bolts 3" long with washers and nuts, hang the board supports (E, F) at desired heights on the uprights (B).

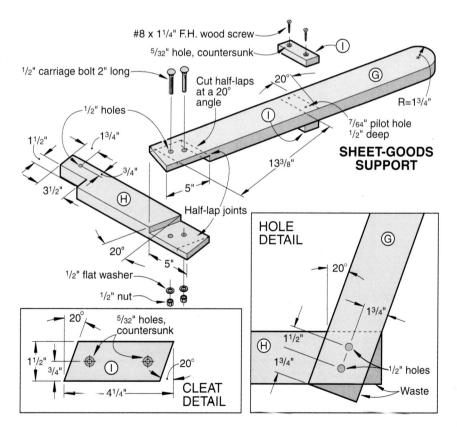

#8 x 1¼" F.H. wood screw

5/32" hole, countersunk

½" carriage bolt 2" long

½" holes

1½"   1¾"

3½"   ¾"

20°

Cut half-laps at a 20° angle

R=1¾"

7/64" pilot hole ½" deep

13⅜"

5"

Half-lap joints

SHEET-GOODS SUPPORT

H

20°

5"

½" flat washer

½" nut

HOLE DETAIL

G

20°

1¾"

H

1½"

1¾"

½" holes

Waste

CLEAT DETAIL

20°

5/32" holes, countersunk

1½"

¾"

I

20°

4¼"

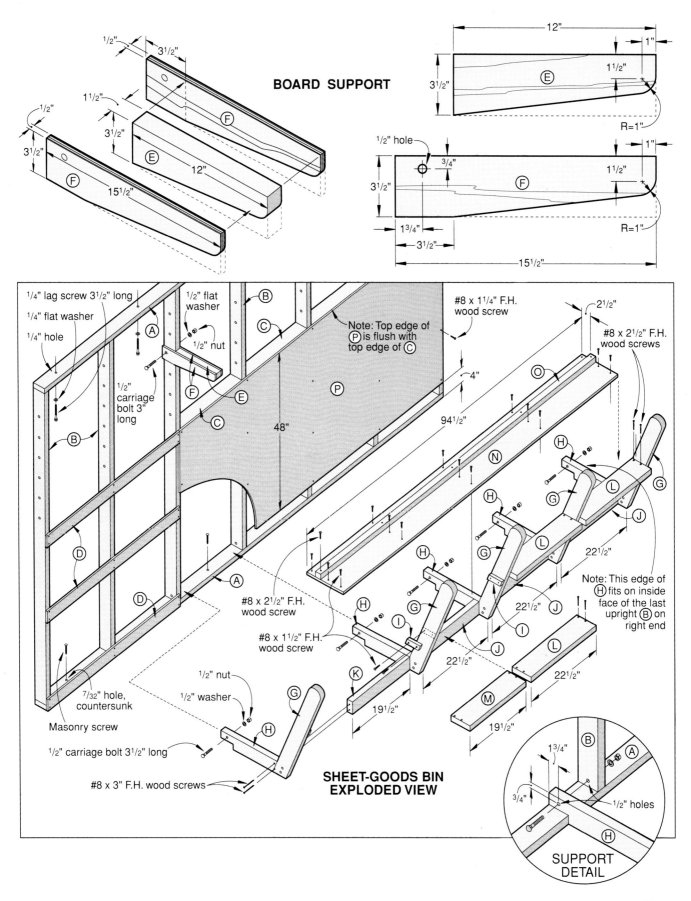

BOARD SUPPORT

E

12"

3½"

1½"

1"

R=1"

½" hole

¾"

3½"

F

1½"

1"

1¾"

3½"

R=1"

15½"

½"

3½"

½"

3½"

1½"

3½"

F

E

12"

½"

3½"

F

15½"

¼" lag screw 3½" long

¼" flat washer

¼" hole

½" flat washer

½" nut

A

B

C

Note: Top edge of P is flush with top edge of C

#8 x 1¼" F.H. wood screw

2½"

#8 x 2½" F.H. wood screws

4"

O

½" carriage bolt 3" long

F

E

C

P

48"

94½"

N

B

H

H

G

G

L

J

D

G

L

22½"

Note: This edge of H fits on inside face of the last upright B on right end

D

H

I

G

J

7/32" hole, countersunk

#8 x 2½" F.H. wood screw

#8 x 1½" F.H. wood screw

H

I

22½"

J

Masonry screw

½" carriage bolt 3½" long

½" nut

½" washer

G

H

K

22½"

19½"

L

22½"

M

19½"

#8 x 3" F.H. wood screws

SHEET-GOODS BIN EXPLODED VIEW

B

A

1¾"

¾"

½" holes

H

SUPPORT DETAIL

GREAT ORGANIZERS FOR YOUR SHOP TOOLS

Here's an even dozen of the handiest shop organizers you'll ever find. All *WOOD*® originals, these easy-to-build projects will put your tools in the right place: at your fingertips when you need them. Good looking and practical, these racks and holders will provide a custom-made home for all your tools, from chisels to wrenches, pliers to saws, and lathe tools to planes. There's even a customized holder to keep your cordless drill and its bits organized.

Quick-as-a-wink chisel rack

Sometimes the best ideas are also the simplest. For this handy little shop project, we went to our scrap pile for the material and invested about a half hour of shop time. Now, we have a topnotch rack for our chisel set.

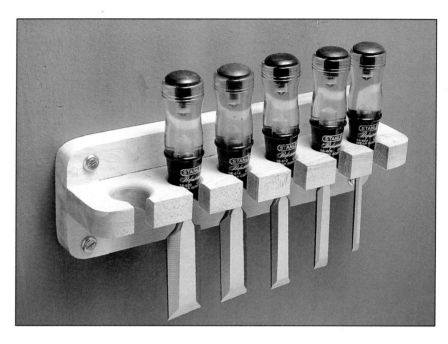

Note: *All stock is ¾" thick. Hole sizes may vary with different brands of chisels.*

Ready wrench rack

We built our racks to handsomely hold a 16-piece (¼" to 1¼") Stanley combination wrench set. As described below and on the drawing in the bottom right corner, you may need to change a few dimensions for your particular set. Also, depending upon how much space you have for hanging your wrenches, you may want to place the racks end to end as shown in the photo *opposite*, or hang one rack under the other.

Note: In our research, we discovered that several manufacturers offer slightly different wrench designs and sell sets containing varying numbers of wrenches. For this reason, the size and number of openings in the racks you make may need to differ from the ones shown here.

continued

EXPLODED VIEW

5/32" hole, countersunk on back side

Use anchors if attaching to drywall

#8 × 1½" F.H. wood screw

11½"

5/32" hole

#8 finish washer

¾"

½"

#8 × 1½" F.H. wood screw
All holes (except for the far left one) are ⅞" diameter

2"

1"

1½"

1½"

1¾"

1¾"

11½"

1¾"

1¾"

1½"

1"

3¼"

R = ⅝"

1 1/16" hole

CHISEL RACK

⅛" round-overs on edges of holes only

NOTCH DETAIL

Hole center-point

R = ⅝"

5/16"

5/16"

⅝"

Note: All stock is ¾" thick. Hole sizes may vary with different brands of chisels.

WRENCH RACK

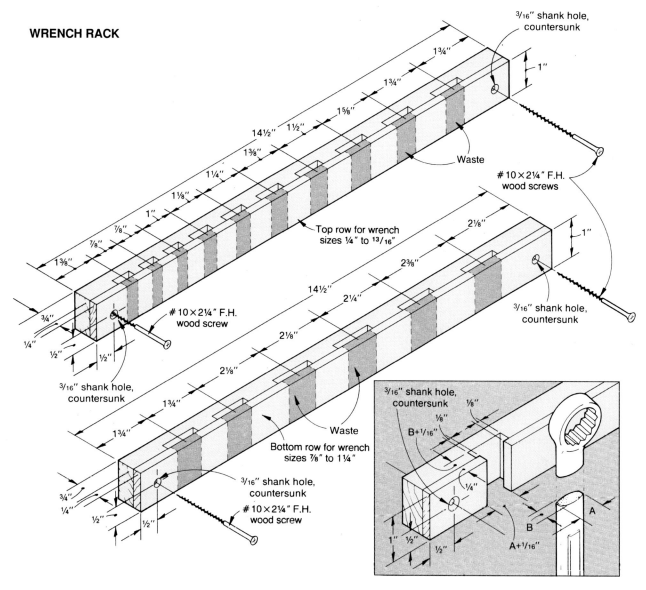

3/16" shank hole, countersunk

1"

1 3/4"

1 3/4"

1 5/8"

1 1/2"

14 1/2"

1 3/8"

1 1/4"

1 1/8"

1"

7/8"

7/8"

1 3/8"

Waste

10 × 2 1/4" F.H. wood screws

Top row for wrench sizes 1/4" to 13/16"

3/4"

1/4"

1/2"

1/2"

3/16" shank hole, countersunk

10 × 2 1/4" F.H. wood screw

2 1/8"

2 3/8"

1"

3/16" shank hole, countersunk

10 × 2 1/4" F.H. wood screws

14 1/2"

2 1/4"

2 1/8"

2 1/8"

1 3/4"

1 3/4"

Waste

Bottom row for wrench sizes 7/8" to 1 1/4"

3/16" shank hole, countersunk

3/4"

1/4"

1/2"

1/2"

3/16" shank hole, countersunk

10 × 2 1/4" F.H. wood screw

3/16" shank hole, countersunk

1/8"

1/8"

B + 1/16"

1/4"

1"

1/2"

1/2"

A + 1/16"

B

A

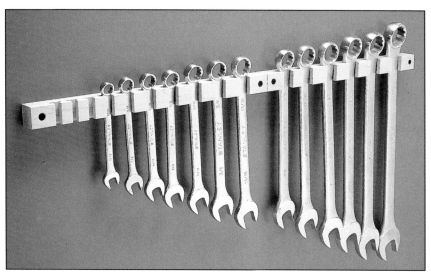

To build the racks, cut the front and back pieces to size. Measure the width (A) of each wrench, and lay out the corresponding dadoes to this width plus 1/16" on the front face of the back pieces. Now measure the thickness (B) of each wrench, and cut the dadoes to this depth plus 1/16".

Glue the pieces together, and then cut away the waste (shaded areas) from the front pieces where shown on the drawings.

GREAT ORGANIZERS FOR YOUR SHOP TOOLS
continued

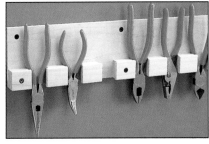

PLIERS RACK

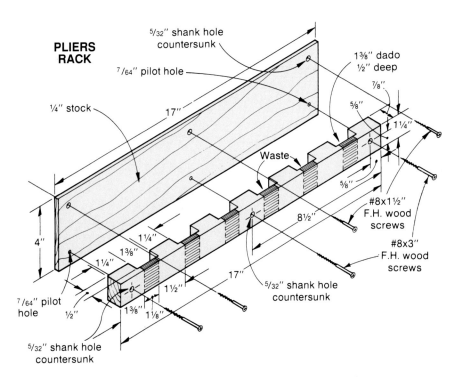

- ⁵/₃₂″ shank hole countersunk
- ⁷/₆₄″ pilot hole
- ¼″ stock
- 17″
- 1³/₈″ dado ½″ deep
- ⁷/₈″
- ⁵/₈″
- 1¼″
- Waste
- 4″
- ⁵/₈″
- #8x1½″ F.H. wood screws
- 1¼″
- 1³/₈″
- 8½″
- #8x3″ F.H. wood screws
- 1¼″
- 1½″
- 17″
- ⁵/₃₂″ shank hole countersunk
- ⁷/₆₄″ pilot hole
- ½″
- 1³/₈″
- 1⅛″
- ⁵/₃₂″ shank hole countersunk

Handy home for a family of pliers

With this nifty, wall-hung organizer, you'll know exactly where to find those bent-nose pliers—or any others—the next time you need them. To build the maple rack, cut the front and back pieces to the sizes shown on the drawing. (We resawed 1¹/₁₆″-thick stock for the ⅞″-thick front piece.) Cut the 1³/₈″ dadoes ½″ deep in the back side of the front piece where marked on the drawing. Glue and screw the two pieces together, flush along the bottom edge. Then, cut the waste (shaded areas) away from the front piece where shown.

The all-business bandsaw blade holder

Protect and store your blades with this handy organizer made from ¼″ birch plywood. After

EXPLODED VIEW

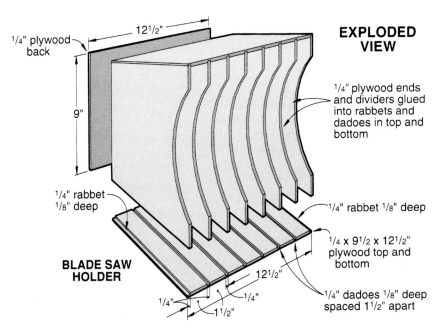

- ¼″ plywood back
- 12½″
- 9″
- ¼″ rabbet ⅛″ deep
- **BLADE SAW HOLDER**
- ¼″
- 1½″
- 12½″
- ¼″
- ¼″ plywood ends and dividers glued into rabbets and dadoes in top and bottom
- ¼″ rabbet ⅛″ deep
- ¼ x 9½ x 12½″ plywood top and bottom
- ¼″ dadoes ⅛″ deep spaced 1½″ apart

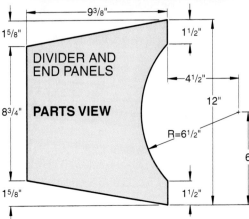

DIVIDER AND END PANELS

PARTS VIEW

- 9³/₈″
- 1⅝″
- 1½″
- 4½″
- 8¾″
- 12″
- R=6½″
- 6″
- 1⅝″
- 1½″

cutting the parts and gluing them together, we mounted the holder to our bandsaw base. Or, you can fasten the organizer to a wall or cabinet side.

Saw-blade selector

Wall-mount this handy holder near the stationary saws in your shop, or if you like, place it on a convenient benchtop. You'll find it the ideal storage project for organizing an assortment of saw blades and a dado-blade set.

To make the notches, cut the side pieces to shape, and mark the notch locations. Then, mount a ¼" dado blade 45° from center, and using your miter gauge with an attached auxiliary wood fence for support, make the cuts.

Simple saw rack

Tired of hanging your handsaws on pegboard hooks or worse, nails? If so, dress up your shop with this sturdy maple organizer. As shown on the drawing, we used ⅛"-thick spacers between the supports for regular handsaws, and ⅜" spacers for backsaws. For safety, hang your saws with the teeth facing the wall.

continued

SAW BLADE SELECTOR

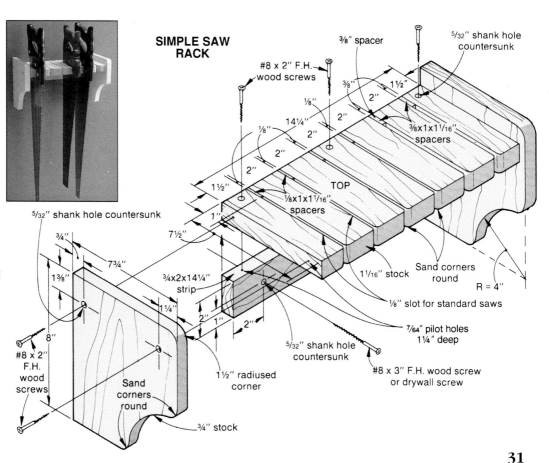

SIMPLE SAW RACK

GREAT ORGANIZERS FOR YOUR SHOP TOOLS
continued

Lathe tool rack

We've always had a problem with long-handled lathe tools toppling off vertical racks. That's why we designed this wall-hung organizer with a tray for turning accessories: It's a sensible way to protect our tool investment.

Note: *This rack is made for tools 19" and longer. If your turning tools are shorter, reduce the width of the entire rack to support your tools.*

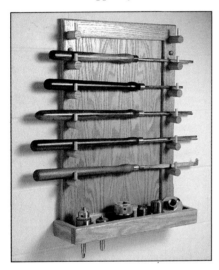

Cordless-drill organizer

Keep your cordless drill, charger, and bits close at hand—without sacrificing valuable work space—with this wall-hung rack.

Build as shown *right*. To fasten the charger to the top shelf, remove the screws securing the feet to the charger case and replace them with longer ones of the same diameter.

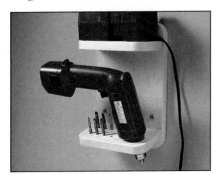

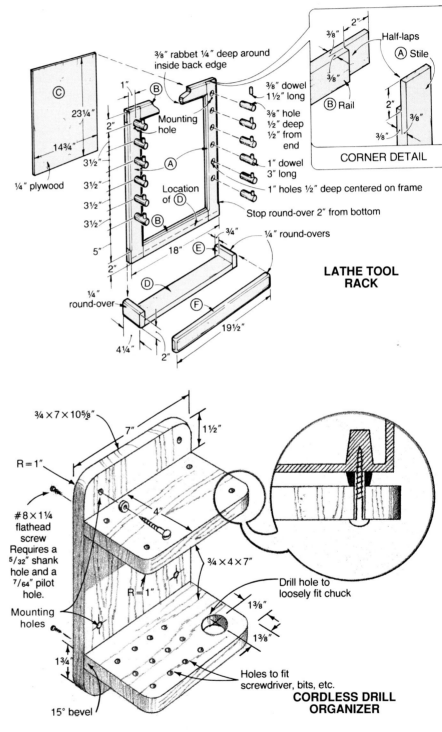

Plain-handy plane holder

Like all precision tools in the shop, your planes need and deserve safe, sturdy storage. Consider this adaptable wall-hung organizer the answer, regardless of which size planes you may own. Using the design shown and the notes *below*, you can build these holders from scrapwood. Then, secure them to your shop wall. We included a dado in the base (A) to protect the plane from damage.

Note: *Length of A equals length of plane plus ½". Length of B equals length of A plus 1½". Width of A and C equals width of plane plus ½". Center the dado in A under plane blade.*

Scrollsaw-blade organizer

Scrollsawers know that laying their hands on the right blade can be tricky and time-consuming, especially if these tiny cutting tools get mixed together. This handy little organizer ends those hassles in a hurry by separating and storing your blades. And all you need

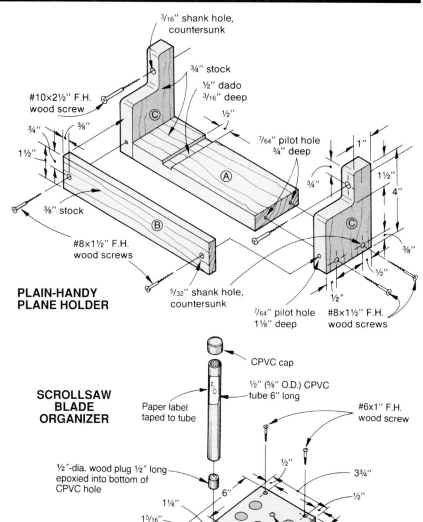

PLAIN-HANDY PLANE HOLDER

- ³⁄₁₆″ shank hole, countersunk
- #10×2½″ F.H. wood screw
- ¾″ stock
- ½″ dado ³⁄₁₆″ deep
- ¾″
- ³⁄₈″
- 1½″
- ³⁄₈″ stock
- ⁷⁄₆₄″ pilot hole ¾″ deep
- #8×1½″ F.H. wood screws
- ⁵⁄₃₂″ shank hole, countersunk
- ¾″
- 1″
- 1½″
- 4″
- ³⁄₈″
- ½″
- ⁷⁄₆₄″ pilot hole 1⅛″ deep
- #8×1½″ F.H. wood screws
- A B C

SCROLLSAW BLADE ORGANIZER

- CPVC cap
- ½″ (⅝″ O.D.) CPVC tube 6″ long
- Paper label taped to tube
- #6×1″ F.H. wood screw
- ½″-dia. wood plug ½″ long epoxied into bottom of CPVC hole
- 1⅛″
- 1⁵⁄₁₆″
- ¾″
- 1⅛″
- 6″
- ½″
- 3¾″
- ½″
- ¼″
- Hole sized to fit scrollsaw tool
- ¹¹⁄₁₆″ holes
- ⁹⁄₆₄″ shank hole, countersunk
- ³⁄₃₂″ pilot hole ½″ deep
- #8×2″ F.H. wood screw
- ⅝″ holes ¼″ deep Note: Hole locations are the same as those in the top pieces.
- ⁹⁄₆₄″ shank hole, countersunk from the bottom
- #6 × 1″ F.H. wood screws
- ⁵⁄₃₂″ hole, countersunk
- ½x3¾x6″ back (optional) used to hang organizer
- #6x1″ F.H. wood screw
- All stock is ½″ thick
- 2¾″
- 6″
- 1⅛″
- 3¾″

to build it is a small amount of scrap stock and some ½"-diameter (⅝" O.D.) CPVC pipe and caps.

For still more convenience, drill a few extra holes in the rack top to hold your scrollsaw tools. Consider labeling the tubes for easy reference. You can hang the unit on a wall or set it on a flat surface near your scrollsaw.

continued

GREAT ORGANIZERS FOR YOUR SHOP TOOLS
continued

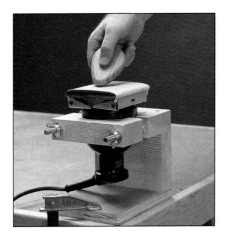

Palm-sander holder

Trying to hold a palm sander in one hand and a small project in the other can make you feel a bit like a juggler. Our holder clamps firmly to your workbench, allowing you to see your sanding progress while leaving both hands free to control the workpiece. For a proper fit, measure the shape of your sander's motor housing to determine the opening size.

To make changing sandpaper a breeze, leave enough clearance between the palm-sander pad and the top of the holder to allow you to change sandpaper without having to remove the sander.

To fit the Porter Cable 330 shown, we cut a 4" hole in a 6x6⅝" block and trimmed the block to the size shown. Hole sizes will vary for other brands of sanders.

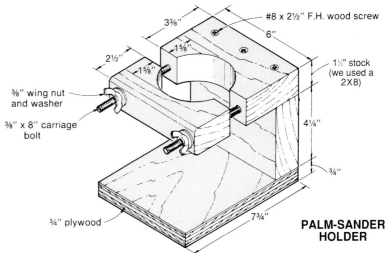

PALM-SANDER HOLDER

- #8 x 2½" F.H. wood screw
- 3⅜"
- 6"
- 2½"
- 1⅝"
- 1⅝"
- 1½" stock (we used a 2X8)
- ⅜" wing nut and washer
- ⅜" x 8" carriage bolt
- 4¼"
- ¾"
- ¾" plywood
- 7¾"

HARDWARE HAULER

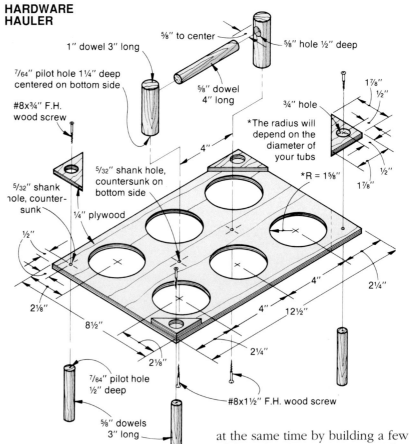

- 1" dowel 3" long
- ⅝" to center
- ⅝" hole ½" deep
- 7/64" pilot hole 1¼" deep centered on bottom side
- ⅝" dowel 4" long
- ¾" hole
- #8x¾" F.H. wood screw
- 1⅞"
- ½"
- ½"
- *The radius will depend on the diameter of your tubs
- *R = 1⅝"
- 1⅞"
- 5/32" shank hole, countersunk on bottom side
- 4"
- 5/32" shank hole, countersunk
- ¼" plywood
- ½"
- 2¼"
- 4"
- 4"
- 12½"
- 2⅛"
- 8½"
- 2¼"
- 2⅛"
- 7/64" pilot hole ½" deep
- #8x1½" F.H. wood screw
- ⅝" dowels 3" long

Handy hardware hauler

Isn't it time you got your nuts and bolts together? Organize your hardware and do a bit of recycling at the same time by building a few of these handy carriers. Perfect for wood buttons, dowel pins, and other small parts, they're stackable too. You'll need several margarine tubs, ¼" plywood, dowels, and wood screws.

ON-THE-GO GLUE CADDY

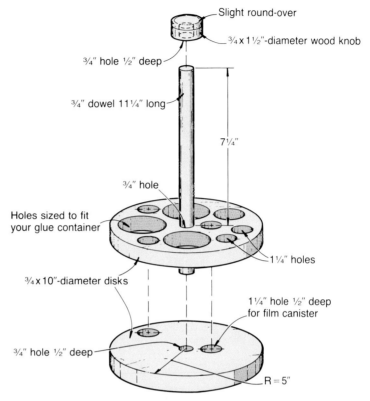

Slight round-over

¾ x 1½"-diameter wood knob

¾" hole ½" deep

¾" dowel 11¼" long

7¼"

¾" hole

Holes sized to fit
your glue container

1¼" holes

¾ x 10"-diameter disks

1¼" hole ½" deep
for film canister

¾" hole ½" deep

R = 5"

Need to get your shop better organized? If so, there's no better place to start than by making our handy glue caddy. It's a cinch to build, and it won't even put a dent in your scrap pile.

Forming the disks

1. Cut two pieces of ¾" stock (we used a pine 1×12) to 11" square. If you don't have stock this wide, laminate narrower pieces.

2. Find the center of one of the squares by marking diagonals. Mark a 10"-diameter circle at the center.

3. Stick the two squares together, marked circle up, with double-faced tape. Cut the disks to shape.

4. Arrange your glue bottles and accessories on top of the disks. Trace around each container. (We added 35mm film canisters for holding cotton swabs, brushes, and other items used to apply glue into those hard-to-get-at places. We also included a foam cup for soaking the glue brushes after each use.)

5. To prevent drilling into your drill press table, mount a piece of scrap material to it. Drill a ¾" hole through the center of both disks. Then, if you plan on using the film canisters as shown in the photograph, switch bits, and drill 1¼" holes through the first disk and ½" deep into the second (we used a

Forstner bit). Separate the disks, and remove the tape.

6. With the 1¼" bit still chucked to your drill press, drill holes through the top disk for additional film canisters. Now, using a circle cutter or hole saw, bore the larger holes as shown in the photo at *right*. Bore through the top disk and just a fraction into the scrap top mounted to your drill press table. Sand both disks and the openings smooth.

Finishing up

1. Cut a piece of ¾" dowel stock 11¼" long for the handle.

2. Slide the top disk onto the ¾" dowel, and position its top face 7¼" down from the top end of the dowel. Mark the position of the disk (top and bottom) on the dowel. Slide the disk away from the marked area, and apply glue between the marked lines on the dowel. Now, slide the disk back onto the glued area, turn it upside

We used a circle cutter for cutting the larger-diameter holes.

down, and run a small bead of glue around the dowel below the top disk. Later, after the top disk is firmly glued in place, glue the dowel into the ¾" hole in the base disk, aligning the holes in the disks.

3. Mark a 1½" circle on a piece of ¾" stock for the knob. Bore a ¾" hole ½" deep at the centerpoint. Cut the knob to shape on a bandsaw, sand smooth, and glue it to the top end of the dowel. Apply a clear finish to all the parts.

ACCESSORIES FOR YOUR SHOP

If your shop is your pride, then this series of projects is for you. Designed to make a workplace run more smoothly, efficiently, and safely, here are pieces so terrific that you'll wonder how you ever worked without them.

A WORKHORSE OF A WORKBENCH

Our Idea-Shop™ workbench may be the design you've waited years for. It's simple to build and super strong. We relied on inexpensive lumberyard stock and rugged mortise-and-tenon joinery to construct the base. For the benchtop, we laminated maple to handle a lifetime of workshop activity. And we added bench dogs and a bench vise to expand the usefulness of our workbench, making it a fitting centerpiece for any home workshop. Plus, see the matching stool on *page 43*.

Let's build the super-sturdy legs first

1. From 1½"-thick, straight-grained pine, rip and crosscut eight pieces 3¼" wide by 33¼" long for the leg blanks. Plane the edges of the stock before ripping it to finished width to remove the rounded corners. (See the box *above right* for our method of obtaining straight-grained pieces from common lumberyard 2×10 stock.)

2. Cut a 3" dado ½" deep 18¾" from the bottom end of each leg blank where shown on the Mortise detail accompanying the End Frame Assembly drawing.

3. Cut a 1×3×6" spacer to temporarily fit in the mating dadoes of two leg blanks where shown on the drawing at *right*. With the spacer between the pair of dadoes and the edges of the leg blanks flush, glue and clamp the pieces together. Then, remove the spacer before the glue dries. (We used pieces of scrapwood stock between the clamp jaws and legs to prevent the metal jaws from denting the softwood.) Repeat the clamping process for each leg.

continued

Design notes

To keep costs down on this project, we hand-picked straight-grained pine 2×10s for the workbench base at a local lumberyard. In addition, we checked each 2×10 for twist and bow, and chose the straightest and driest pieces available. (If you have a moisture meter, take it with you when you shop.)

After getting the stock back to the *WOOD*® magazine shop, we stickered the boards, and let them acclimate to our indoor environment for several weeks before cutting the parts (A, B, C, D) from along the edges where shown in the sketch at *right*. This allowed us to use the straightest grain possible and achieve the best results.

Joint edges to remove rounded corners

Cut parts from straight grain

2 x 10 x 12'

For even drying, place strips of wood underneath stock to allow air to pass freely around board

Pith

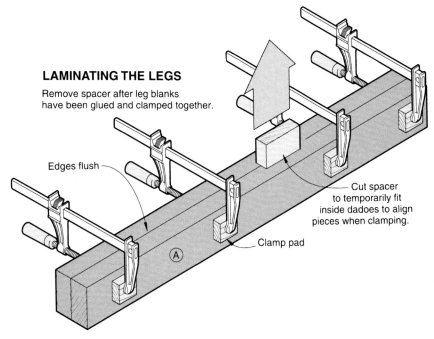

LAMINATING THE LEGS

Remove spacer after leg blanks have been glued and clamped together.

Edges flush

Cut spacer to temporarily fit inside dadoes to align pieces when clamping.

Clamp pad

A

A WORKHORSE OF A WORKBENCH

continued

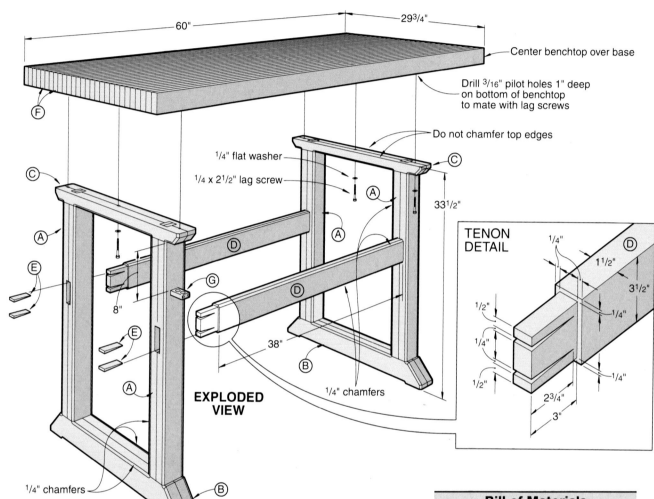

Center benchtop over base

Drill 3/16" pilot holes 1" deep on bottom of benchtop to mate with lag screws

Do not chamfer top edges

1/4" flat washer

1/4 x 2 1/2" lag screw

33 1/2"

8"

38"

1/4" chamfers

1/4" chamfers

EXPLODED VIEW

TENON DETAIL

1/4"

1 1/2"

3 1/2"

1/4"

1/2"

1/4"

1/4"

1/2"

1/4"

2 3/4"

3"

CUTTING DIAGRAM

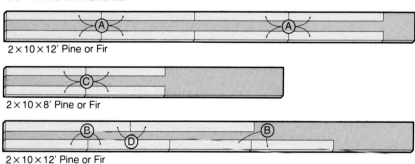

2 × 10 × 12' Pine or Fir

2 × 10 × 8' Pine or Fir

2 × 10 × 12' Pine or Fir

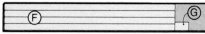

1 1/16 x 9 1/4 x 72" Maple (7 pieces)

Bill of Materials

Part	Finished Size			Mat.	Qty.
	T	W	L		
A* legs	3"	3"	33 1/4"	LP	4
B* feet	3"	3 1/4"	29 1/2"	LP	2
C* rails	3"	1 1/2"	28"	LP	2
D stretchers	1 1/2"	3 1/2"	44"	P	2
E* wedges	3/8"	1"	3 1/4"	DH	8
F* top pieces	1 1/16"	2 1/4"	60"	M	28
G dog holder	1 1/16"	1 3/4"	2 5/8"	M	1

*Initially cut parts marked with an * oversized. Then, trim each to finished size according to the how-to instructions.

Material Key: LP—laminated pine, P—pine, DH—dark hardwood, M—maple

Supplies: 3—1/2" all-thread rods 27 1/4" long, 6—1/2" nuts, 6—1/2" flat washers, 6—1/4X2 1/2" lag screws, 1/4" flat washers, clear finish.

4. Remove the clamps, scrape the glue from one edge, and plane ⅛" from the scraped edge to get it flat. Rip the opposite edge for a 3¹⁄₁₆" width. Next, plane ¹⁄₁₆" from the cut edge to remove the saw marks and to obtain the 3" finished width. Repeat for each leg.

Now, add the feet and rails for a wobble-free base

1. For the feet (B) and the rails (C), see the End-Frame Assembly on *page 40* and Parts View drawings on *page 41*, follow the same method described to form the legs (A). Cut the pieces oversized in width, cut the dadoes, glue the pieces together with the dadoes and edges of the boards aligned, and then trim to finished width.

2. Clamp the two feet (B) bottom edge to bottom edge. Mark a centerpoint 3¼" from each end of the clamped-together feet. Now, use a compass to mark a ½" hole (¼" radius) at each centerpoint. Draw straight lines to connect the edges of each circle where shown in Photo A *above*.

3. Mark a 45° cutline across the end of each leg where shown on the Parts View drawing. Do the same thing to the ends of the rails where shown on the End-Frame Assembly drawing.

4. As shown in Photo A, drill a ½" hole at each marked centerpoint. Remove the clamps, and bandsaw between the holes along the inside edge of the marked line. Sand to the line to remove saw marks.

5. Using the dimensions on the End-Frame Assembly and Parts View drawings, miter-cut (we used a bandsaw) both ends of each foot (B) and both ends of each rail (C). Sand smooth.

6. Drill a trio of ⅜" holes in each rail (C) where shown on the Parts View drawing.

Next, let's assemble the base

1. Mount an auxiliary wood fence to your miter gauge and a dado blade to your tablesaw. Cut tenons to the sizes shown on the *continued*

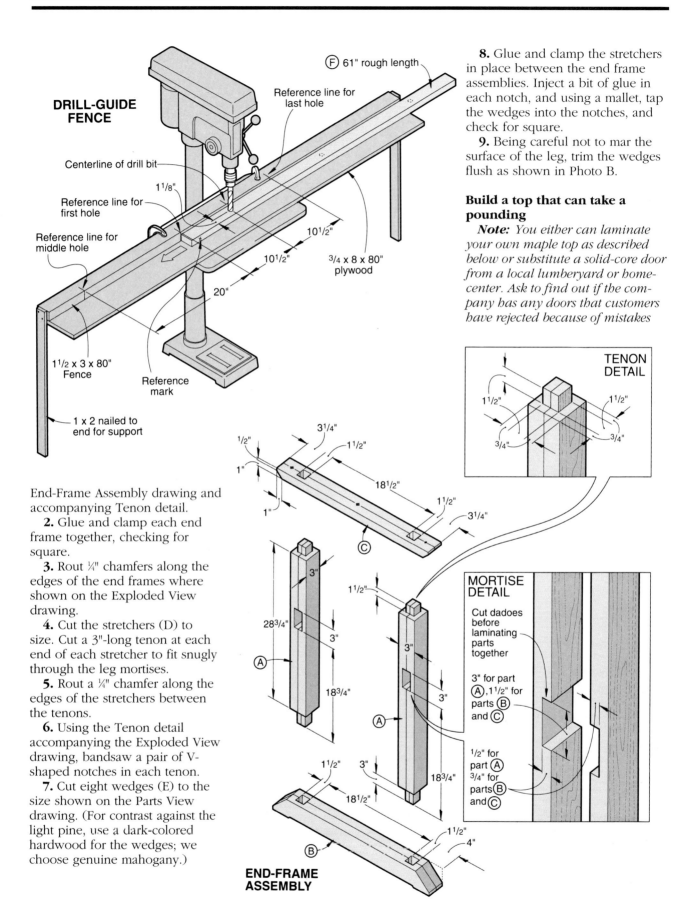

DRILL-GUIDE FENCE

F 61" rough length

Reference line for last hole

Centerline of drill bit

1¹/₈"

Reference line for first hole

Reference line for middle hole

10¹/₂"

10¹/₂"

³/₄ x 8 x 80" plywood

20"

1¹/₂ x 3 x 80" Fence

Reference mark

1 x 2 nailed to end for support

End-Frame Assembly drawing and accompanying Tenon detail.

2. Glue and clamp each end frame together, checking for square.

3. Rout ¼" chamfers along the edges of the end frames where shown on the Exploded View drawing.

4. Cut the stretchers (D) to size. Cut a 3"-long tenon at each end of each stretcher to fit snugly through the leg mortises.

5. Rout a ¼" chamfer along the edges of the stretchers between the tenons.

6. Using the Tenon detail accompanying the Exploded View drawing, bandsaw a pair of V-shaped notches in each tenon.

7. Cut eight wedges (E) to the size shown on the Parts View drawing. (For contrast against the light pine, use a dark-colored hardwood for the wedges; we choose genuine mahogany.)

8. Glue and clamp the stretchers in place between the end frame assemblies. Inject a bit of glue in each notch, and using a mallet, tap the wedges into the notches, and check for square.

9. Being careful not to mar the surface of the leg, trim the wedges flush as shown in Photo B.

Build a top that can take a pounding

Note: You either can laminate your own maple top as described below or substitute a solid-core door from a local lumberyard or home-center. Ask to find out if the company has any doors that customers have rejected because of mistakes

TENON DETAIL

1¹/₂"   1¹/₂"

³/₄"   ³/₄"

3¹/₄"

¹/₂"

1¹/₂"

1"

18¹/₂"

1"

1¹/₂"

3¹/₄"

C

3"

28³/₄"

A

18³/₄"

1¹/₂"

A

1¹/₂"

3"

18¹/₂"

B

3"

3"

3"

A

18³/₄"

1¹/₂"

4"

END-FRAME ASSEMBLY

MORTISE DETAIL

Cut dadoes before laminating parts together

3" for part A, 1¹/₂" for parts B and C

¹/₂" for part A ³/₄" for parts B and C

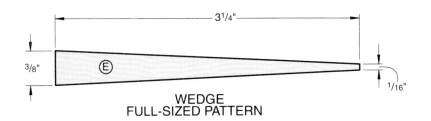

**WEDGE
FULL-SIZED PATTERN**

$3^1/4$"

$3/8$"

$1/16$"

E

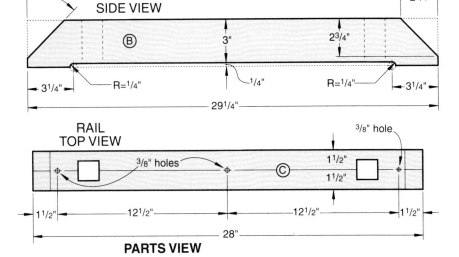

**FOOT
SIDE VIEW**

45°

$2^3/4$"

B

3"

$2^3/4$"

$3^1/4$"

R=$1/4$"

$1/4$"

R=$1/4$"

$3^1/4$"

$29^1/4$"

**RAIL
TOP VIEW**

$3/8$" hole

$3/8$" holes

C

$1^1/2$"

$1^1/2$"

$1^1/2$"

$12^1/2$"

$12^1/2$"

$1^1/2$"

28"

PARTS VIEW

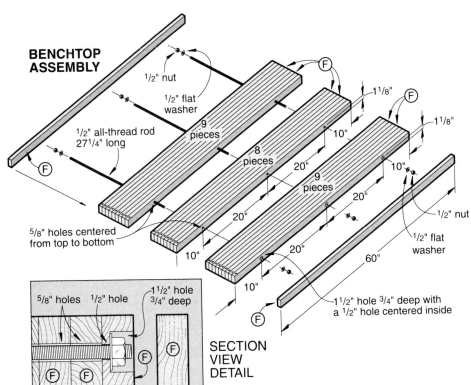

**BENCHTOP
ASSEMBLY**

$1/2$" nut

$1/2$" flat
washer

$1/2$" all-thread rod
$27^1/4$" long

9
pieces

$1^1/8$"

F

$1^1/8$"

F

10"

8
pieces

20"

10"

9
pieces

$1/2$" nut

20"

$1/2$" flat
washer

$5/8$" holes centered
from top to bottom

10"

20"

10"

60"

$1^1/2$" hole $3/4$" deep with
a $1/2$" hole centered inside

F

F

F

F

$5/8$" holes $1/2$" hole

$1^1/2$" hole
$3/4$" deep

F

F

F

**SECTION
VIEW
DETAIL**

*in staining or cutting. You can
purchase these for a fraction of
their retail cost. Avoid doors
rejected because of warpage.*

1. Cut 28 pieces of $1^1/16$"-thick
maple (F) to $2^1/8$x61" for the laminated top. For reference when
drilling and laminating later, mark
an **X** on the best (defect-free) edge
(not face) of each strip.

2. Using the drawing on *page
40, top* for reference, construct
and attach a long fence to your
drill press to ensure consistently
spaced holes. Add a support to
each end. Mark the reference
marks on the fence where shown
on the drawing.

3. With the marked edge facing
out, align the ends with the reference marks on the fence, and drill
three $5/8$" holes in 24 of the 28
benchtop pieces (F).

4. Still using the fence and your
marks, drill three $1^1/2$" holes $3/4$" deep
with a $1/2$" hole centered inside each
$1^1/2$" hole in two of the remaining
four pieces.

5. Glue and clamp eight of the
predrilled pieces (F) face-to-face,
with the edges and ends flush, the
$5/8$" holes aligned, and the **X**s facing
up. Next, glue and clamp two nine-
piece sections together in the same
manner. Each of the nine-piece
sections should have a strip with
the $1^1/2$" holes on one outside edge.
See the Top Assembly drawing for
reference. (We found it easier to
laminate three sections, and then
glue and clamp the three sections
together to form the top.) You
should still have two maple strips
(F) with no holes in them.

6. Using a hacksaw, cut three
pieces of $1/2$"-diameter all-thread
rod to $27^1/4$" long.

7. Spread glue on the mating
edges, and clamp the three sections
edge-to-edge, using pipe clamps
and the all-thread rod with nuts
continued

A WORKHORSE OF A WORKBENCH

continued

and flat washers attached. Check that the surfaces are flush. (We used a ratchet to tighten the ½" nuts on the all-thread rod.) Alternate back and forth between the clamps and the nuts on the threaded rods for even clamping pressure.

8. Glue the remaining two top pieces (F) to the edges of the top assembly to hide the holes and threaded rods.

9. Scrape off the excess glue, and then belt-sand both surfaces of the benchtop flat.

10. Fit your portable circular saw with a carbide-tipped blade. Clamp a straightedge to the benchtop, and trim ½" off one end of the benchtop. Repeat at the other end.

Finishing up

1. Finish-sand the base and top.

2. Center the benchtop assembly on the base. Clamp the top to the base. Using the previously drilled holes in the rails (C) as guides, drill six ⁵⁄₁₆" pilot holes 1" deep into the bottom side of the benchtop assembly. The holes in the rail are slightly oversized to allow the lag screws to move with the expansion and contraction of the benchtop. Using ¼" lag screws and flat washers, fasten the base to the top.

3. Add the finish to all surfaces. (We applied three coats of Watco Natural Danish Oil Finish.)

4. Drill the mounting holes, and add a vise using the instructions provided with the vise (see the Buying Guide for our source).

5. Measure your bench-dog diameter. Then, mark and drill the dog holes through the benchtop where shown in the drawing *below.*

6. If you use the same type of round bench dogs we did, mark the layout for the dog holder (G) on a piece of 1¹⁄₁₆" maple. Mark the centerpoints for the dogs and the mounting screws. Bore the holes for the dogs, and then cut the dog holder to shape. Next, drill the mounting holes, sand smooth, and apply the finish. Finally, screw the dog holder to the leg nearest the vise.

Buying Guide

• **Woodworker's Vise.** Cast-iron jaws, predrilled mounting holes, 34 lbs., with retractable "dog," Catalog No. 9GT51785. Available at or order through Sears stores nationwide.

• **Round bench dogs.** Two, with wire springs allowing for height adjustment. Catalog No. 827116. For current prices, contact Woodworker's Supply, Inc., 5604 Alameda Place NE, Albuquerque, NM 87113, or call 800-645-9292 to order.

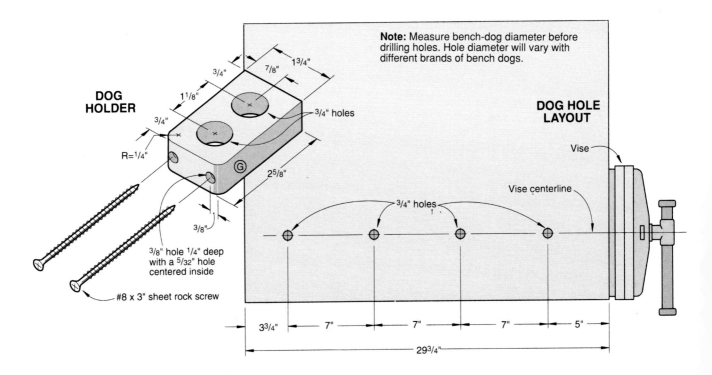

SIT-A-SPELL SHOP STOOL

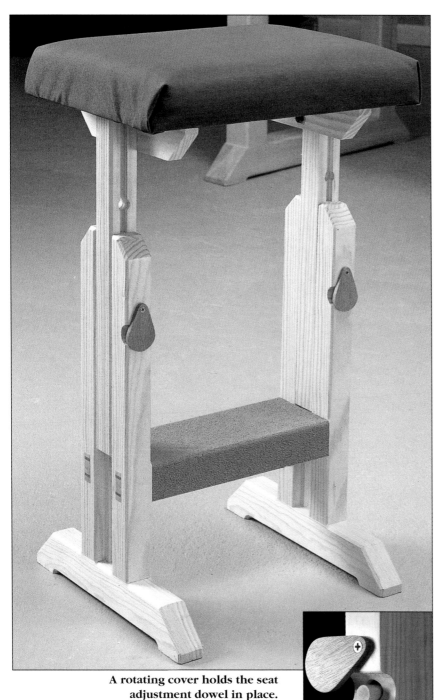

A rotating cover holds the seat
adjustment dowel in place.

If you're one of those woodworkers who spends every
spare minute working in your
shop, you're going to love this
shop stool. The padded seat
makes it a joy to sit on. And with
the special height-adjustment
system we've designed into it,
you can raise or lower the seat
to suit your height and the
surface you're working at.

Cut and laminate pieces for the legs, feet, and stretchers

1. To form the laminated legs
(A), cut eight pieces of ¾"-thick
straight-grained pine (we used
1×4s) to 1¾" wide by 19" long
for the leg blanks.

2. Cut a 1½" dado ¼" deep 8" from
the bottom end of each leg where
shown on Leg drawing on *page 46.*

3. Cut a ⅜×1½×3" spacer to
temporarily fit in the mating dadoes
of two leg blanks. With the spacer
between the dadoes and the edges
of the leg blanks flush, glue and
clamp the pieces. Immediately after
clamping, remove the spacer
Repeat for the other three legs.

4. Remove the clamps, scrape the
glue from one edge, and plane the
scraped edge to get it flat. Then, rip
the opposite edge for a 1⁹⁄₁₆" width.
Next, plane ¹⁄₁₆" from the cut edge to
remove the saw marks and obtain
the 1½" finished width. Repeat for
the other legs.

5. Follow the method described
in Steps 1–4 above to make the feet
(B). Cut the pieces oversized in
width, cut the dadoes, glue the
pieces together, and then trim.
Repeat the process (minus the
dadoes) for the stretchers (C).

Finish machining the legs, feet, and stretchers

1. Mount an auxiliary wood
fence to your miter gauge and a
dado blade to your tablesaw. Using
the dimensions on the Tenon detail
accompanying the Stretcher
Assembly drawing, cut tenons on
continued

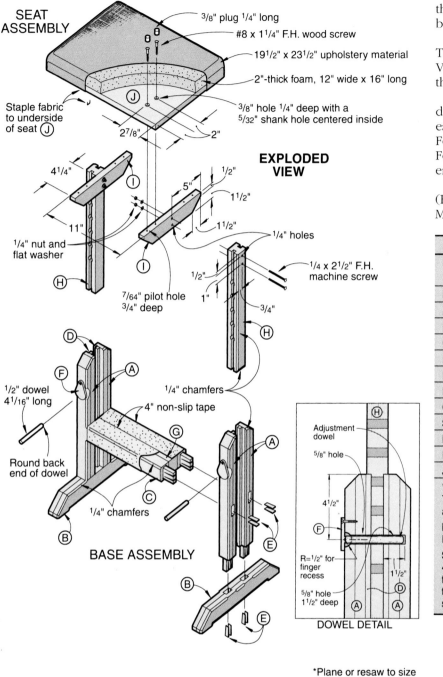

SEAT ASSEMBLY

3/8" plug 1/4" long

#8 x 1 1/4" F.H. wood screw

19 1/2" x 23 1/2" upholstery material

2"-thick foam, 12" wide x 16" long

3/8" hole 1/4" deep with a 5/32" shank hole centered inside

Staple fabric to underside of seat ⓙ

ⓙ

2 7/8" 2"

EXPLODED VIEW

4 1/4"

ⓘ

5" 1/2"

1 1/2"

11"

1 1/2"

1/4" nut and flat washer

ⓘ 1/4" holes

ⓗ

1/4 x 2 1/2" F.H. machine screw

1/2" 1/2"

1"

3/4"

7/64" pilot hole 3/4" deep

ⓗ

ⓓ

ⓕ ⓐ

1/2" dowel 4 1/16" long

1/4" chamfers

4" non-slip tape

ⓖ

ⓐ

Round back end of dowel

ⓒ

1/4" chamfers

ⓑ

BASE ASSEMBLY

ⓔ

ⓑ

ⓔ

DOWEL DETAIL

ⓗ

Adjustment dowel

5/8" hole

4 1/2"

ⓕ

R=1/2" for finger recess

5/8" hole 1 1/2" deep

1 1/2"

ⓓ

ⓐ ⓐ

the bottom ends of the legs and both ends of the stretchers.

2. Using the dimensions on the Tenon detail, bandsaw a pair of V-shaped notches in each tenon in the stretchers and legs.

3. With the dimensions on the Leg drawing, angle-cut the top end of each leg. Use the dimensions on the Foot drawing and accompanying Foot End detail to angle-cut both ends of each foot.

4. Clamp (without glue) the feet (B) bottom edge to bottom edge. Mark a centerpoint 2¼" from each

Bill of Materials

Part	Finished Size			Mat.	Qty.
	T	**W**	**L**		
BASE ASSEMBLY					
A* legs	1½"	1½"	19"	LP	4
B* feet	1½"	2¼"	14"	LP	2
C* stretchers	1½"	2"	14"	LP	2
D guides	⅜"	⅜"	17"	P	4
E wedges	⁵⁄₁₆"	½"	2¼"	DH	16
F covers	¼"	1⅜"	2¼"	DH	2
G* spacer	1½"	2"	11"	LP	1
SEAT ASSEMBLY					
H* posts	1½"	1½"	17"	LP	2
I rails	¾"	2"	10"	P	2
J* seat	¾"	12"	16"	EJP	1

*Initially cut parts marked with an * oversized. Then, trim each part to the finished size according to the how-to instructions.

Material Key: LP—laminated pine, P—pine, DH—dark hardwood, EJP—edge-joined pine

Supplies: #8X1¼" flathead wood screws, 4–¼X2½" flathead brass machine screws with flat washers and nuts, ½" dowel stock, nonslip tape, 2"-thick foam, upholstery material, staples, clear finish.

*Plane or resaw to size listed in Bill of Materials.

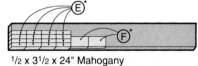

ⓔ*

ⓕ*

1/2 x 3 1/2 x 24" Mahogany

CUTTING DIAGRAM

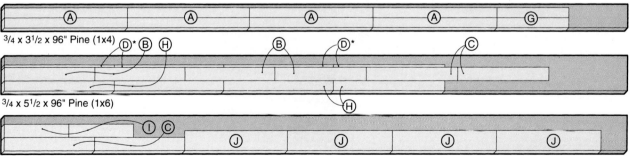

ⓐ   ⓐ   ⓐ   ⓐ   ⓖ

3/4 x 3 1/2 x 96" Pine (1x4)

ⓓ* ⓑ ⓗ   ⓑ   ⓓ*   ⓒ

3/4 x 5 1/2 x 96" Pine (1x6)

ⓗ

ⓘ ⓒ

ⓙ   ⓙ   ⓙ   ⓙ

3/4 x 5 1/2 x 96" Pine (1x6)

end of the legs. Use a compass to mark a ½" hole at each centerpoint. Draw lines to connect the edges of each marked circle.

5. Drill a ½" hole at each marked centerpoint. Remove the clamps, and bandsaw out the waste between the holes, cutting just inside the marked lines. Sand to the lines to remove the saw marks and finish shaping each recess.

It's time to assemble the stool base

1. Cut the four guides (D) to the size stated in the Bill of Materials. With the ends flush and the guide centered from side to side, glue and clamp one guide to each leg. See the Guide detail accompanying the Leg drawing for reference.

2. Transfer the full-sized wedge pattern (E) to ½"-thick dark hardwood (we chose mahogany), and cut 16 wedges to shape.

3. Next, transfer the hole cover pattern (F) and hole centerpoint to ¼"-thick stock. Cut the covers to shape, drill and countersink a ⁵⁄₃₂" mounting hole in each, and set them aside for now. Fastened to the legs later, the covers prevent the dowels from sliding out when you move the stool around.

4. To bore the adjustment-dowel holes, dry-clamp a pair of legs together with the tenoned ends flush and the guides (D) mating and flush. Using a brad-point bit, bore a ⅝" hole where shown in the Dowel detail accompanying the Exploded View drawing and the Leg drawing. Drill through the first leg/guide and 1½" into the second leg/guide.

5. To form the finger recesses, clamp the two front legs with the bored sides face to face, holes aligned, and the tenoned ends flush. Drill a 1" hole 4½" from the top end and centered over the ⅝" adjustment-dowel holes as shown in the photo *right*.

6. Glue and clamp the stretchers (C) between the legs (A), checking for square. Inject a bit of glue in
continued

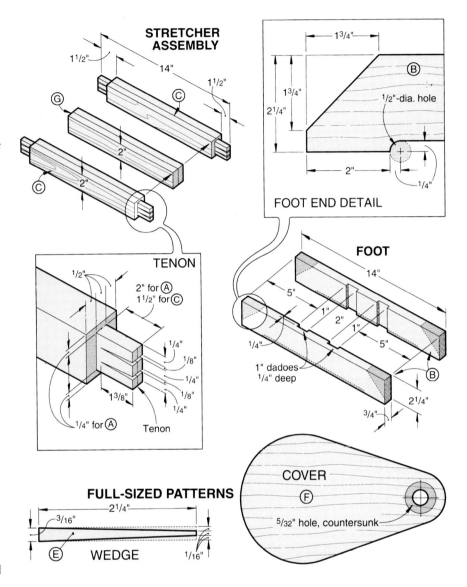

With the stool legs clamped together and the adjustment-dowel holes aligned, bore a 1" hole through both legs to form the finger recesses.

SIT-A-SPELL SHOP STOOL

continued

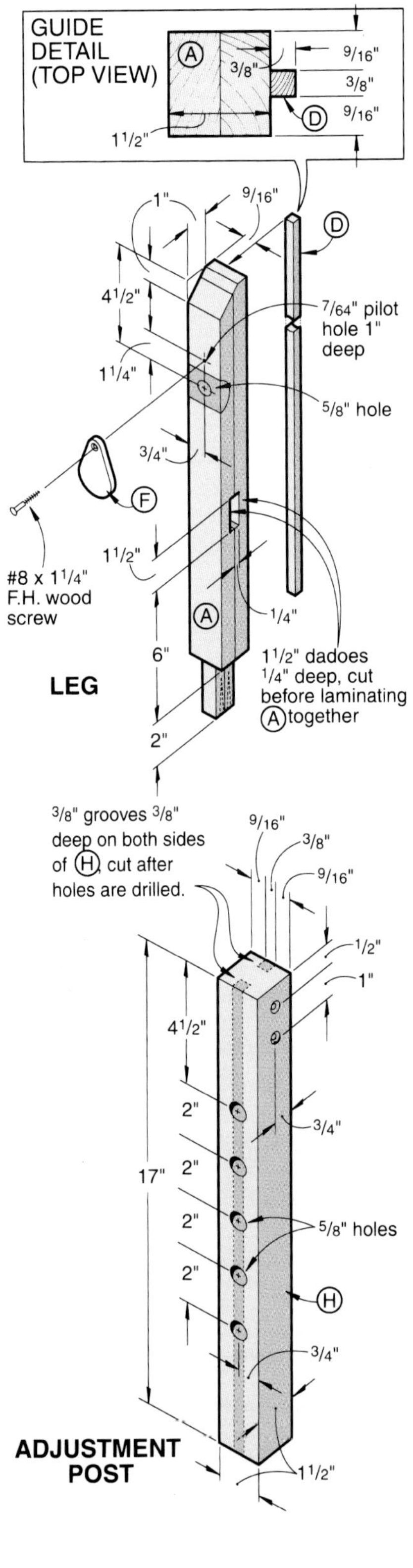
GUIDE DETAIL (TOP VIEW)
A
3/8"
9/16"
3/8"
9/16"
D
1 1/2"
1"
9/16"
D
4 1/2"
7/64" pilot hole 1" deep
1 1/4"
5/8" hole
3/4"
F
#8 x 1 1/4" F.H. wood screw
1 1/2"
A
1/4"
6"
1 1/2" dadoes 1/4" deep, cut before laminating A together
LEG
2"
3/8" grooves 3/8" deep on both sides of H cut after holes are drilled.
9/16"
3/8"
9/16"
1/2"
1"
4 1/2"
2"
3/4"
17"
2"
2"
5/8" holes
2"
H
3/4"
ADJUSTMENT POST
1 1/2"

each notch, and using a mallet, tap the wedges into the notches. Again, check for square.

7. Glue and clamp the feet (B) to the bottom ends of the legs (A). Glue and drive the wedges.

8. Being careful not to mar the surfaces of the leg, trim and sand the wedges flush.

9. Measure the opening between the stretchers (C), and cut the spacer (G) to fit. (Since we were already using ¾" stock, we laminated two pieces and then trimmed the laminated piece to size.) Glue the spacer in place.

10. Rout ¼" chamfers along the edges of the base pieces where shown on the Exploded View drawing.

Let's add the adjustable seat

1. Laminate ¾" stock, and trim the adjustment posts (H) to size.

2. Mark the centerpoints for the ⅝" holes on the surface (not edge) where shown on the Adjustment Post drawing, and bore the five holes through each post.

3. Rout ¼" chamfers along the edge and bottom ends where shown on the Exploded View drawing.

4. Cut or rout a ⅜" groove ⅜" deep centered over the ⅝" holes on both sides of each post. Test the fit of each post on the guides between each pair of legs; the posts should slide easily up and down on their mating guides. If not, slightly enlarge the grooves.

5. Cut the seat rails (I) to size, angle-cutting the ends where dimensioned on the Exploded View drawing. Drill a pair of ¼" holes through each rail where shown on the Adjustment Post drawing.

6. Edge-join ¾" stock, and cut the seat (J) to size.

7. With the top edges flush, glue a rail to the inside face of each post (H), checking for square. Using the previously drilled ¼" holes in the rails as guides, drill ¼" holes through the posts. Strengthen each rail/post joint with a pair of ¼x2½" flathead machine screws.

8. Cut a pair of ½" dowels 4$\frac{1}{16}$" long. For easy insertion into the legs later, sand a round-over on one end of each dowel.

Fasten the seat to the adjustable posts

1. Insert the adjustment posts between the legs, adjust to the same level, and insert the dowels.

2. Center, then glue and clamp the seat to the rails.

3. To further secure the seat to the rails, drill eight ⅜" holes ¼" deep where shown on the Exploded View drawing, centered over the rails. Drill a shank hole through the seat and a pilot hole into the rail as dimensioned on the Exploded View. Drive #8x1¼" wood screws through the holes.

4. Using a ⅜" plug cutter, cut eight plugs from $\frac{5}{16}$" stock. Glue the plugs in place, and sand the protruding ends of the plugs flush with the top surface of the seat.

Clean up before taking a seat

1. Disassemble the loose parts and sand the base, seat assembly, and covers (F) smooth.

2. To protect the stretchers, apply nonslip tape.

3. Mask the nonslip tape, and apply a clear finish to the parts (we used satin polyurethane).

4. For an exposed wood seat, rout a ⅜" round-over along the seat's top edge. Or, for a cushioned seat, have a piece of 2"-thick foam cut to size, cover it with upholstery material, and staple the material to the bottom of the seat.

5. Slide the seat assembly's adjustment posts into the base. Fasten the covers (F) to the base. Raise the stool to a comfortable seating height, insert the dowels, and give yourself a well-deserved break.

LABOR-OF-LOVE WORKBENCH

Before designing this workbench, I talked to numerous woodworkers to determine what features they wanted. Then, I headed for the drawing board. Our bench has a base that can be kept simple like the one in the inset photo. Or, build the one *above* with doors and drawers. I've also incorporated a large 30×60" worktop, a bench-dog-and-vise system, and a board jack (see *page 55*).

—*J. R. Downing*
Design Editor

Note: For the frame members (parts A, B, C, E, F) we used 1½" birch. To save money, you could substitute pine, fir, or spruce 2x4s and 2x6s for these parts.

Let's start with the end panels

1. Cut the end panel uprights (A) and rails (B, C) to the sizes listed in the Bill of Materials.

2. Set a stop, and cut half-laps on the ends of each upright and rail. See the End Panel drawing *page 48, top left* for reference.

3. Glue and clamp together each end frame, checking for square.

Later, scrape off the excess glue and sand both end frames.

4. Mark the centerpoints for eight ¾" holes on the *outside* face of each end frame (see the End Panel drawing for hole locations). Set a stop for consistent depths, and bore ¾" holes ⅜" deep at each marked centerpoint. (See the Corner detail on *page 48* for reference.) Switch bits, and drill a ¼" hole through the stock, centered inside each ¾" hole, backing the stock with scrap to prevent chip-out.

5. Rout a ½" rabbet along the *inside* face of each end frame where shown on the End Panel drawing.
continued

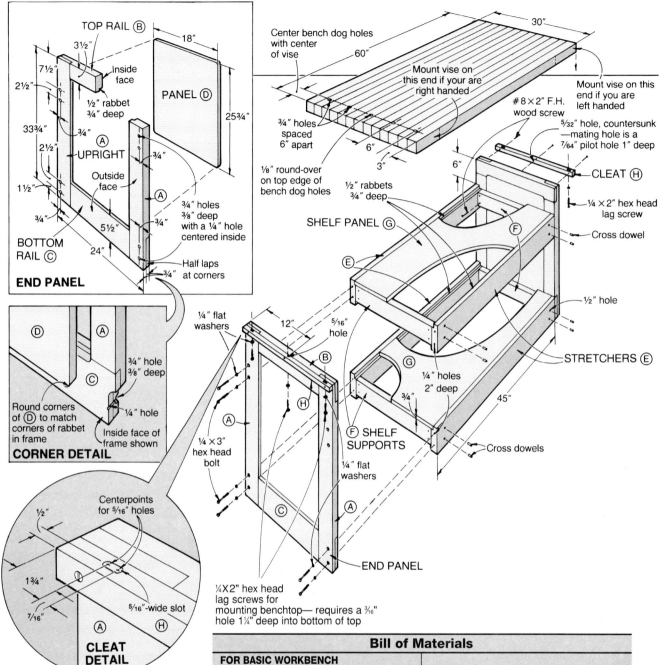

END PANEL

TOP RAIL Ⓑ

3½"

7½"

2½"

33¾"

2½"

1½"

¾"

Inside face

½" rabbet ¾" deep

PANEL Ⓓ

18"

25¾"

¾"

Ⓐ

Ⓐ UPRIGHT

¾"

Outside face

Ⓐ

¾"

5½"

24"

BOTTOM RAIL Ⓒ

¾"

¾" holes ⅜" deep with a ¼" hole centered inside

Half laps at corners

CORNER DETAIL

Ⓓ Ⓐ

Ⓒ

¾" hole ⅜" deep

¼" hole

Round corners of Ⓓ to match corners of rabbet in frame

Inside face of frame shown

CLEAT DETAIL

Centerpoints for 5/16" holes

½"

1¾"

7/16"

5/16"-wide slot

Ⓐ Ⓗ

Center bench dog holes with center of vise

60"

30"

Mount vise on this end if your are right handed

Mount vise on this end if you are left handed

¾" holes spaced 6" apart

6"

3"

⅛" round-over on top edge of bench dog holes

#8 × 2" F.H. wood screw

5/32" hole, countersunk —mating hole is a 7/64" pilot hole 1" deep

½" rabbets ¾" deep

SHELF PANEL Ⓖ

Ⓔ

Ⓕ

CLEAT Ⓗ

¼ × 2" hex head lag screw

Cross dowel

½" hole

STRETCHERS Ⓔ

12"

5/16" hole

Ⓑ

Ⓖ

¼" holes 2" deep

45"

¾"

¼" flat washers

¼ × 3" hex head bolt

Ⓐ

Ⓗ

Ⓕ SHELF SUPPORTS

¼" flat washers

Ⓒ

Ⓐ

END PANEL

¼X2" hex head lag screws for mounting benchtop— requires a 3/16" hole 1¼" deep into bottom of top

6. Measure the rabbeted openings, and cut two pieces of ¾" plywood (D) to size. Cut or sand the square corners of the plywood panels to fit into the rounded corners of the rabbets in the end frames. Glue and clamp the plywood panels into the rabbets, and remove any excess glue with a damp cloth.

Bill of Materials

FOR BASIC WORKBENCH										
Part	Finished Size			Mat.	Qty.	Part	Finished Size			Mat.	Qty.
	T	W	L				T	W	L		
A uprights	1½"	3½"	33¾"	B	4	K jaw liners	¾"	2¾"	7⅛"	B	2
B top rails	1½"	3½"	24"	B	2	L removable strip	¾"	1¾"	52⅞"	B	1
C bottom rails	1½"	5½"	24"	B	2						
D panels	¾"	18"	25¾"	BP	2						
E stretchers	1½"	5½"	45"	B	4						
F shelf supports	1½"	3½"	21"	B	4						
G shelf panels	¾"	22"	45"	BP	2						
H cleats	1"	1"	24"	B	2						
I spacer block	1¹/₁₆"	4"	6½"	B	1						
J* facing strip	⅝"	1¾"	52⅞"	B	1						

*Initially cut the part marked with an * oversized. Trim it to finished size according to the how-to instructions.

Material Key: B–birch, BP–birch plywood

Supplies: #8X2" flathead wood screws, ¼X2" lag screws, ⅜ X4" flathead machine screws with washers and nuts, 5/16 X1" flathead machine screws, ¾" dowel stock, ¼X3" hexhead bolts with flat washers, clear finish.

Add the stretchers for stability

1. Cut the stretchers (E) to size.

2. Cut a ½" rabbet ¾" deep on the top inside edge of each stretcher. (We cut ours on the tablesaw with a dado blade; a table-mounted router fitted with a fence and straight bit also would work.)

3. Mark the locations, and dry-clamp the stretchers in place between the end panels where shown on the drawing *below*.

4. Using the previously drilled holes in the end-panel uprights as guides, drill a pair of ¼" holes 2" deep into the ends of each stretcher as shown *below*. (If your bit is too short, drill as deep as you can and finish drilling the holes to 2" deep after removing the clamps in the next step.)

5. With the stretchers still dry-clamped in place, and using the drawing *below* for reference, mark matching numbers and location reference lines on each stretcher end and mating upright for relocating the stretchers later. Remove the clamps and finish drilling the ¼" holes to 2" deep into the ends of each stretcher.

6. Following the three-step drawing *above right,* mark the centerpoints for the cross-dowel holes. (When assembling the workbench later, the ¼x3" bolt threads into the cross dowels to hold the assembly together.) Then, drill ½" holes through the stretchers where marked, backing the stock with scrap to prevent chip-out.

7. Dry-clamp the stretchers (in the same location as before) between the end panels. Insert ¼" cross dowels into the ½" holes (see

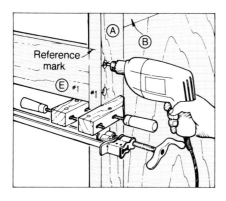

Reference mark

the Buying Guide for our source of hardware). Bolt the end panels to the stretchers with ¼x3" hex-head bolts. (See the drawing *below right* for reference.) Thread the bolts through the cross dowels. (Be careful not to overtighten the bolts; we snapped off the head of one bolt.)

Now, for the shelves

1. Measure the distance between the stretchers (E), and cut the shelf supports (F) to size. Glue and screw the supports between the stretchers, with the *top edge* of the supports flush with the *bottom edge* of the rabbet cut in each stretcher. (See the Basic Bench drawing for reference.)

2. Measure the openings, and cut the shelf panels (G) to size. Check the fit, and then glue and clamp the panels into place.

Add the cleats and locate the vise

Note: See the box on page 51 *titled Topping It Off for benchtop alternatives.*

1. Cut the cleats (H) to size. Mark the centerpoints for the ⁵⁄₁₆" holes on the top face of each cleat. (See the Cleat detail accompanying the Basic Bench drawing for the locations of the ⁵⁄₁₆" holes needed to form the slots.) Drill the holes where marked. With a chisel, remove material between holes to form the slots. When fastening the benchtop to the cleats later, the slots allow the benchtop to expand and contract without splitting the cleat or benchtop.

2. With the top edges flush, glue and screw the cleats (H) to the top rail (B) on the outside face of each end panel.

3. Position the benchtop on the base and allow for a 9" overhang on the end on which you mount the vise. If you are right-handed, mount the vise on the left-hand end. If you're left-handed, position the vise on the opposite end (same edge) and leave a 9" overhang on that end.

4. With the benchtop correctly positioned, trace the outline of the bench base on the bottom of the

LOCATING THE THREADED DOWEL HOLES

STEP 1.
Use a try square to mark lines along both sides of each hole.

STEP 2.
Find center between lines and transfer centerlines down outside face.

Centerpoint for ½" hole

1½"

STEP 3.
Measure down 1½" and mark a line across the face of the board

(E)

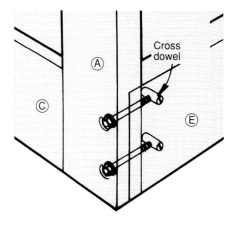

Cross dowel

(A)

(C)

(E)

benchtop for repositioning the benchtop on the base later.

Let's add the vise

Note: If you plan on adding the doors and drawers, do that first, and then add the vise. The instructions for adding the doors and drawers start on page 51.

We cut parts I, J, K, and L to fit the vise and laminated benchtop noted in the Buying Guide. If you use a different vise and top, your dimensions may vary.

1. With the benchtop on the base, cut the spacer (I) to fit between the vise mount and the bottom surface of the benchtop. (See the Vise drawing for reference. To accommodate the mounting bolts, we cut ¾x¾" notches in the back two corners of the spacer.) The thickness of the spacer should drop the top edge of the vise jaws ¹⁄₁₆" *below* the top surface of the benchtop. The thickness

continued

LABOR-OF-LOVE WORKBENCH
continued

of the spacer will depend on the thickness of your benchtop. The $\frac{1}{16}$" gap prevents projects on the benchtop from contacting the metal jaws of the vise.

2. Clamp the vise in position on the bottom surface of the worktop. With a helper, position the benchtop *upside down* on the workbench base.

3. Using the mounting holes in the vise as guides, drill through the spacer block and benchtop, backing what will be the top of the benchtop with scrap to prevent chipout. (See the photo *below*.) Temporarily bolt the vise in place.

Attach the benchtop, and add the facing strips

1. With the aid of a helper, turn the benchtop right side up, and position it on the base, using the previously drawn outline for alignment.

2. Using the slots and holes in the cleats as guides, drill $\frac{5}{16}$" holes 1" deep into the bottom side of the top for the $\frac{1}{4}\times2$" lag screws. Be sure to center the pilot holes in the slots. Screw (but don't glue) the benchtop to the base.

3. Remove the vise, spacer, and mounting screws from the benchtop. So you won't scratch your projects, countersink the vise

With the benchtop upside down, bore the vise-mounting holes through the spacer block and benchtop.

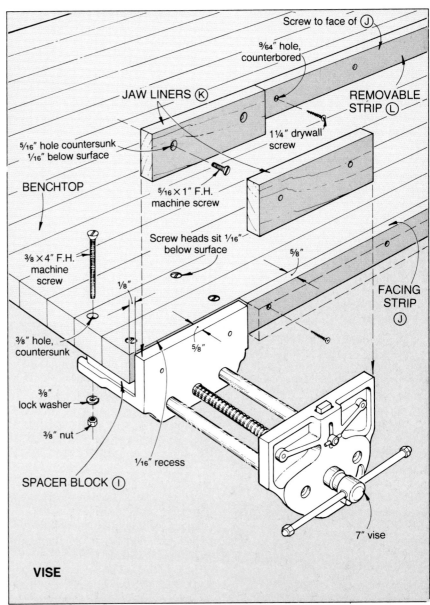

Screw to face of Ⓙ

$\frac{9}{64}$" hole, counterbored

JAW LINERS Ⓚ

REMOVABLE STRIP Ⓛ

$\frac{5}{16}$" hole countersunk $\frac{1}{16}$" below surface

$1\frac{1}{4}$" drywall screw

BENCHTOP

$\frac{5}{16}\times1$" F.H. machine screw

Screw heads sit $\frac{1}{16}$" below surface

$\frac{5}{8}$"

FACING STRIP Ⓙ

$\frac{3}{8}\times4$" F.H. machine screw

$\frac{1}{8}$"

$\frac{3}{8}$" hole, countersunk

$\frac{5}{8}$"

$\frac{3}{8}$" lock washer

$\frac{3}{8}$" nut

$\frac{1}{16}$" recess

SPACER BLOCK Ⓘ

7" vise

VISE

mounting holes so the mounting screws sit $\frac{1}{16}$" below the top surface. With the spacer in place, bolt the vise to the benchtop.

4. Measure the distance from the inside face of the metal vise jaw to the front edge of the benchtop (ours measured $\frac{5}{8}$"). Resaw or plane a 60"-long by $1\frac{3}{4}$"-wide strip (J) to match the measured distance. See the Vise drawing for reference. Cut the strip to length. One end of the strip should fit against the vise jaw; the other end, flush with the end of

the benchtop. Glue and screw the strip to the edge of the benchtop.

5. Cut the vise-jaw liners (K) to size. Using the Vise drawing for reference, drill holes and fasten the liners to the vise jaws.

6. Cut another $1\frac{3}{4}$"-wide strip from $\frac{3}{4}$" stock for the removable strip (L). (We've made the strip removable so it can be replaced should you accidentally saw into it.) Drill and counterbore holes into the removable strip where shown on the Vise drawing. Screw (no glue) the strip to the edge of the benchtop.

Time to drill the dog holes and make the bench dogs

1. Mark the dog hole centerpoints on the benchtop where located on the Exploded View drawing.

2. Build a drill guide like the one shown *top right*. Then, bore ¾" holes into the benchtop as shown *center right*. The guide helps keep the holes perpendicular to the workbench surface. When boring the hole closest to the vise, bore only 1½" deep to avoid hitting the vise mount and damaging the drill bit. Back the bottom of the benchtop with scrap to prevent chip-out.

3. Rout a ⅛" round-over on the top inside edge of each hole.

4. To build a bench dog, cut a 3x3" square from ¾" plywood. Draw diagonal lines on the block, and bore a ¾" hole at the marked centerpoint. Sand a slight round-over on all edges of the block.

5. Cut a ¾" oak dowel to 2½" long. Sand a round-over on the bottom end. Glue the dowel into the hole in the plywood square.

Next, build the drawers

1. Using the Cutting Diagram on *pages 53–54* and the Drawer drawing *below right* for reference, cut a 6" strip off the end of a sheet of ¾" plywood. Cut the drawer fronts (M) to size.

2. From ½" and ¾" plywood, cut the four drawer sides (N), back (O), and bottom (P) to size.

3. Cut a ⅝" rabbet ½" deep along both ends of each drawer front. Machine a ¾" dado ¼" deep 1" from the back edge across each drawer side. Using the Drawer drawing *right* for reference, cut a ½" groove ¼" deep ½" from the bottom edge along the inside face of the drawer front and sides.

4. Dry-clamp the drawers together to check the fit. Trim any parts if necessary. The bottom edge of the drawer front (M) sits ⅛" lower than the bottom edge of the sides (N). Locate the centerpoints on each drawer side, and drill and countersink the holes for the 1½" screws. Remove the clamps.

Topping it off: Let your budget decide

You can top a workbench in several different ways. First, you can cut forty ¾"-thick strips 1¾" wide by 60" long. With the surfaces flush, glue them together face to face in three sections. Then, glue and clamp together the three sections. Next, scrape and belt-sand the lamination smooth to form the benchtop.

You also can purchase damaged solid-core doors at most building supply centers for under $25.

See the Buying Guide on *page 54* for our source of the laminated-maple top used on this workbench.

5. Glue and screw the drawer together, checking for square.

6. Mark the centerpoints for the beech pulls. Drill the holes and fasten a pull to each drawer.

continued

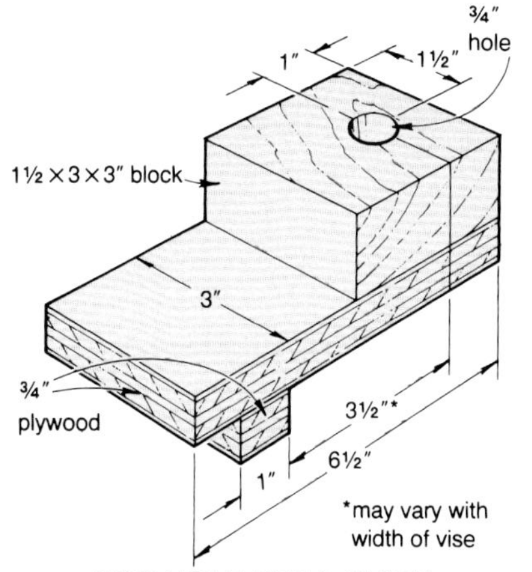
¾" hole
1"
1½"
1½ x 3 x 3" block
3"
¾" plywood
3½"*
6½"
1"
*may vary with width of vise
DOG HOLE DRILL GUIDE

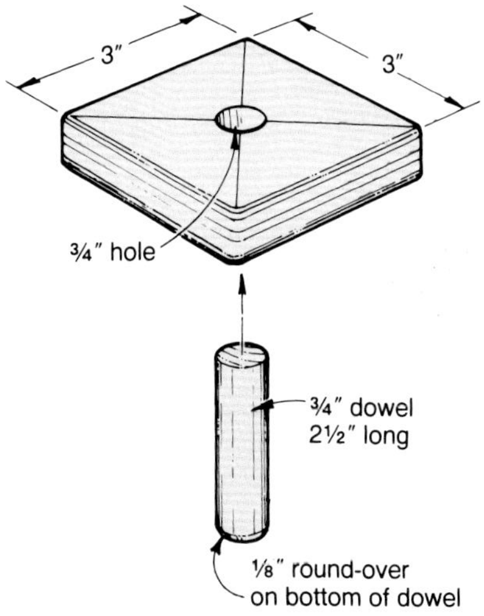
3"
3"
¾" hole
¾" dowel 2½" long
⅛" round-over on bottom of dowel
BENCH DOG

DRAWER

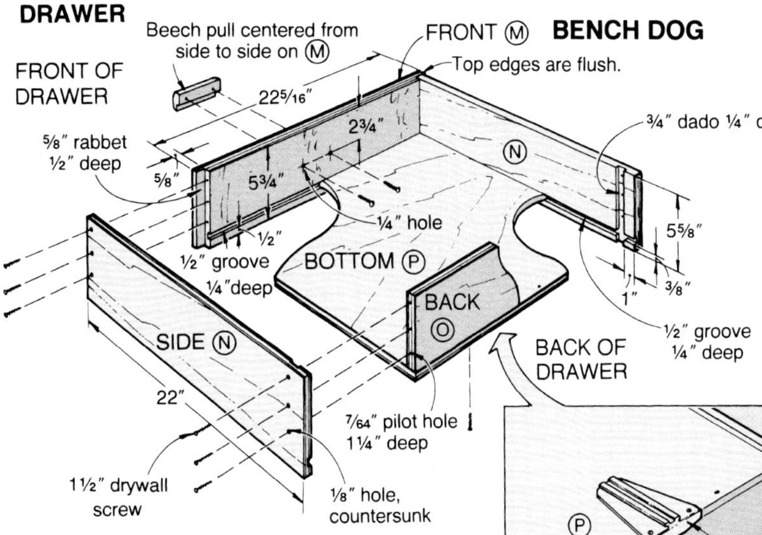
FRONT OF DRAWER
Beech pull centered from side to side on (M)
FRONT (M)
Top edges are flush.
22⁵⁄₁₆"
2¾"
⅝" rabbet ½" deep
⅝"
5¾"
¾" dado ¼" deep
(N)
¼" hole
½"
½" groove ¼"deep
BOTTOM (P)
5⅝"
BACK (O)
1"
⅜"
SIDE (N)
BACK OF DRAWER
½" groove ¼" deep
22"
⁷⁄₆₄" pilot hole 1¼" deep
1½" drywall screw
⅛" hole, countersunk

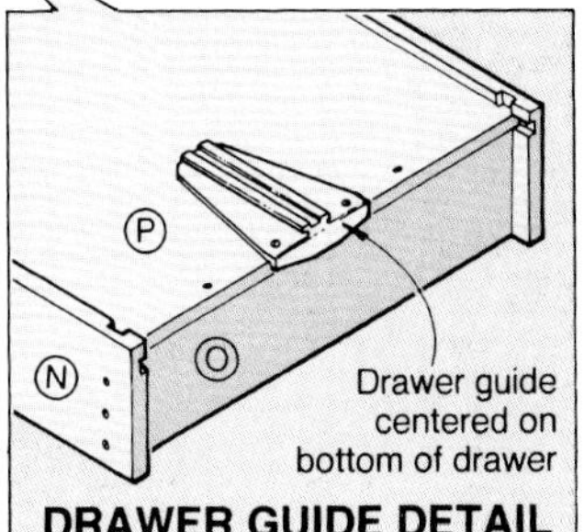
(P)
(N)
(O)
Drawer guide centered on bottom of drawer
DRAWER GUIDE DETAIL

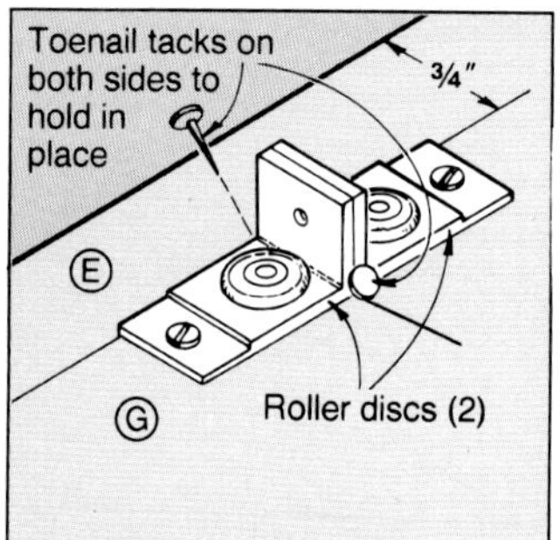

Toenail tacks on both sides to hold in place
3/4"
E
G
Roller discs (2)

ROLLER DETAIL

Bill of Materials

FOR EXPANDED BENCH

Part	Finished Size T	Finished Size W	Finished Size L	Mat.	Qty.
M drawer fronts	¾"	22 5/16"	5¾"	BP	2
N drawer sides	½"	5⅝"	22"	BP	4
O drawer backs	¾"	4¾"	21 9/16"	BP	2
P drawer bottom	½"	20¾"	21 9/16"	BP	2
Q center divider	¾"	21 11/16"	21½"	BP	1
R cleats	¾"	¾"	20 15/16"	B	2
S cleats	¾"	¾"	22⅛"	B	2
T cleats	¾"	¾"	16 "	B	2
U cleats	¾"	¾"	10¼"	B	2
V cleat	¾"	¾"	20½"	B	1
W cleats	¾"	¾"	5¼"	B	2
X top back panel	¾"	45"	6"	BP	1
Y bottom back panel	¾"	45"	16¾"	BP	1
Z doors	¾"	11 3/32"	16½"	BP	4

Material Key: B—birch, BP—birch plywood

Supplies: 1¼" flathead wood screws, #8X2½" flathead wood screws, ¼" flat washers, ¼X3" hexhead bolts, ¼" cross dowels, ¼X2½" lag screws.

EXPLODED VIEW

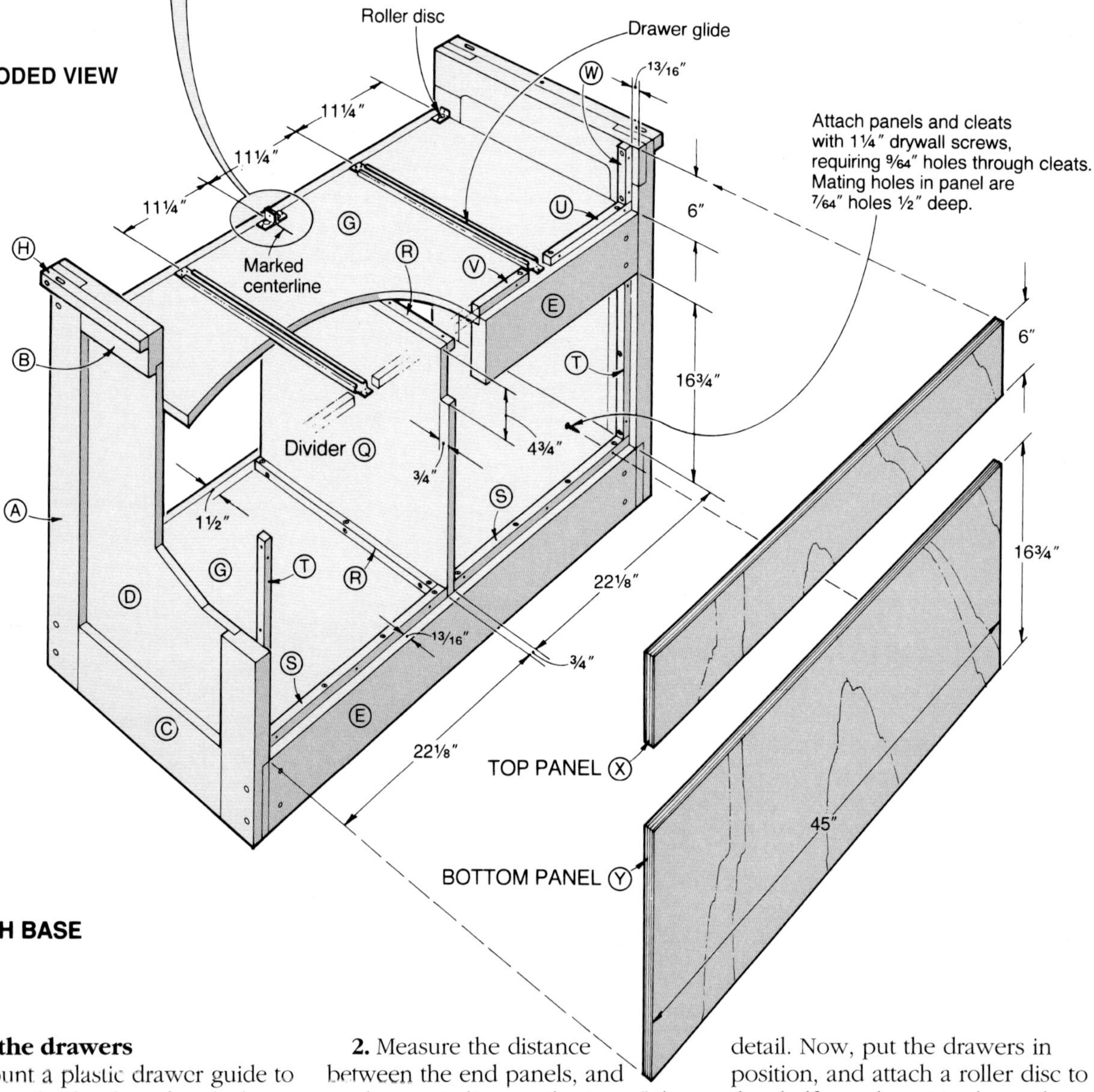

Roller disc
Drawer glide
W
13/16"
11¼"
11¼"
11¼"
Attach panels and cleats with 1¼" drywall screws, requiring 9/64" holes through cleats. Mating holes in panel are 7/64" holes ½" deep.
U
6"
G
H
R
V
Marked centerline
E
B
T
16¾"
6"
Divider Q
4¾"
¾"
S
A
1½"
G
T
R
D
13/16"
22⅛"
¾"
S
E
C
22⅛"
TOP PANEL X
16¾"
45"
BOTTOM PANEL Y

BENCH BASE

Install the drawers

1. Mount a plastic drawer guide to the bottom back edge of each drawer, centered from side to side. (See the Drawer Guide detail accompanying the Drawer drawing for reference.)

2. Measure the distance between the end panels, and mark a centerline on the top of the shelf panel (G) where shown on the Bench Base drawing. Attach a roller on each side of the marked centerline where shown on the Roller detail. Now, put the drawers in position, and attach a roller disc to the shelf panel next to the end panels where shown on the Bench Base drawing.

continued

Locate and clamp the drill guide to the benchtop. Drill ¾" dog holes in the top.

3. Mark a centerline between each set of rollers. Using a square, mark the centerline from the front of the shelf to the back. Position a metal drawer glide over each line, and fasten each glide with just one screw in the middle. Fit both drawers into position and check the alignment of the rollers and glides. Adjust the glides as required. Next, install the rest of the screws to hold the slides in place.

Attach the divider, cleats, and back panels

1. From ¾" plywood, cut the center divider (Q) to fit, cutting a notch for the back stretcher (E).

2. Cut the divider cleats (R) to size. Glue and screw cleats to the top and bottom of the divider panel. Slip the divider into position and screw it to the shelves (G). The divider should be ¹³⁄₁₆" from the back side of the cabinet and 1½" from the front.

3. Cut and install the remaining cleats (S, T, U, V, W) ¹³⁄₁₆" from the backside of the cabinet.

4. Cut the back panels (X, Y) to size. Glue the panels in place.

Add the doors and let's put this bench to work

1. Cut two pieces of ¾" birch plywood to 22⁵⁄₁₆" by 16½" for the four front doors (Z) where shown on the Cutting Diagram. Mark a centerline down the center of each panel. Glue and screw a pull over this centerline where shown on the drawing *right.*

2. Following the marked centerline, and cutting through the center of the pulls, cut each plywood door panel in half.

3. Using the drawing on *page 54, top* for reference, fasten a fixing plate flush with the top and bottom inside corners of each door.

4. Drill the holes in the stretchers (E) for the bushings. (If you need more room when drilling, loosen the hex-head bolts threaded through the cross dowels.) Insert a bushing in each hole. Push the hinges into the bushings, slide the fixing plates (attached to the doors) *continued*

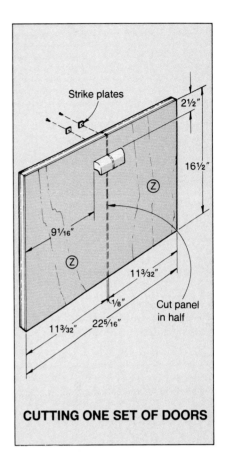

CUTTING ONE SET OF DOORS

CUTTING DIAGRAM

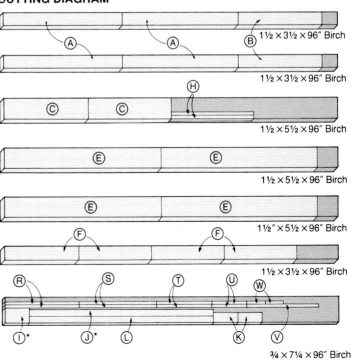

LABOR-OF-LOVE WORKBENCH
continued

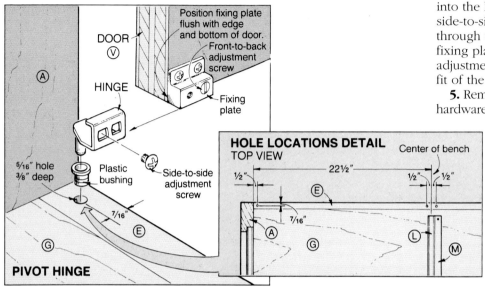

PIVOT HINGE

Position fixing plate flush with edge and bottom of door.

DOOR ⓥ

Front-to-back adjustment screw

HINGE

Fixing plate

Ⓐ

⁵⁄₁₆" hole ³⁄₈" deep

Plastic bushing

Side-to-side adjustment screw

⁷⁄₁₆"

Ⓔ

Ⓖ

HOLE LOCATIONS DETAIL
TOP VIEW

Center of bench

22½"

½"   ½"   ½"

Ⓔ

⁷⁄₁₆"

Ⓐ   Ⓖ   Ⓛ   Ⓜ

into the hinges, and thread the side-to-side adjustment screw through the hinge and into the fixing plate. Position the two adjustment screws for a good fit of the doors.

5. Remove or mask all the hardware. Stain and finish. (We left ours natural—no stain— and applied several coats of polyurethane.) Add the catches to the bottom of the top stretcher. Mark the mating location for the strike plates on the upper corners of each door back and fasten them in place. (See the drawing titled Cutting the Doors for reference when locating the strike plates.)

Buying Guide

• **Hardware.** For the basic bench, order threaded steel cross dowels, Catalog No. D6618 (16 needed). If you're building the workbench with drawers and doors, you'll need the following hardware: 1¼x4" beech pulls, Catalog No. B2527 (four needed). Delta 100 drawer glide with low-friction disc rollers, Catalog No. D8400 (two needed). Pivot hinges and plastic bushing, Catalog No. D5600 (four pair needed). Magnetic catch and strike plates, Catalog No. D2107 (four needed). For current prices, contact The Woodworkers' Store, 21801 Industrial Blvd., Rogers, MN 55374-9514, or call 800-279-4441 or 612-428-2199 to order.

• **Vise.** Cast-iron, lever-type quick release, 3"-deep by 7"-wide jaws, 8" maximum opening, Catalog No. G1091. For current prices, contact Grizzly Imports, P.O. Box 2069, Bellingham, WA 98227, or call 800-541-5537 to order.

• **Laminated maple benchtop.** 1¾x30x60" butcher block, Part No. BB3060. For current prices, contact Dunn and Company, 97 Washington, Des Moines, IA 50314, or call 800-728-3866 to order.

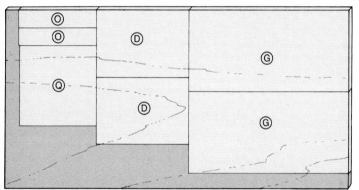

¾ × 48 × 96" Birch Plywood

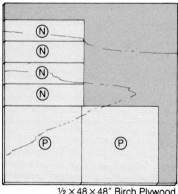

½ × 48 × 48" Birch Plywood

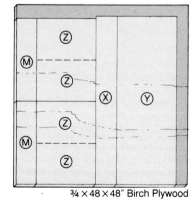

¾ × 48 × 48" Birch Plywood

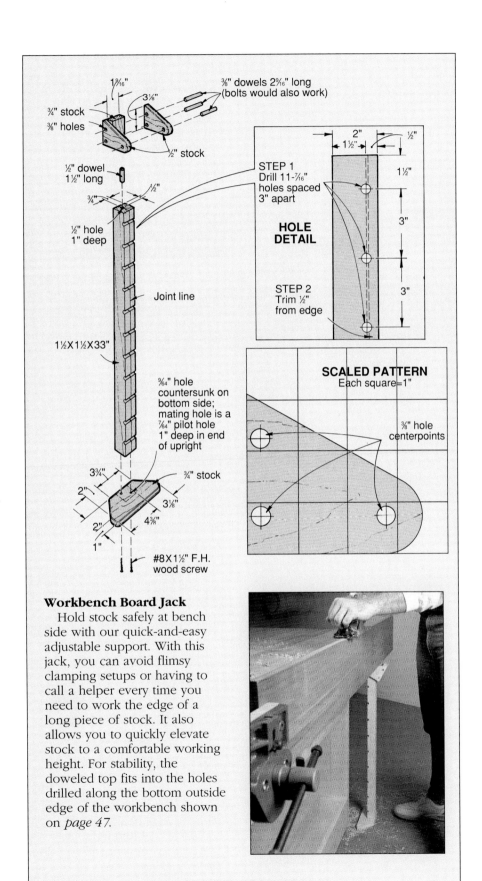

1⅛"

¾" stock
⅜" holes

3⅛"

⅜" dowels 2⁹⁄₁₆" long
(bolts would also work)

½" stock

½" dowel
1½" long

½"

¾"

½" hole
1" deep

Joint line

STEP 1
Drill 11-⁷⁄₁₆"
holes spaced
3" apart

2"   **½"**
1½"   **1½"**

3"

3"

**HOLE
DETAIL**

STEP 2
Trim ½"
from edge

1½X1½X33"

⁹⁄₆₄" hole
countersunk on
bottom side;
mating hole is a
⁷⁄₆₄" pilot hole
1" deep in end
of upright

SCALED PATTERN
Each square=1"

**⅜" hole
centerpoints**

3¾"

2"

2"

1"

¾" stock

3⅛"

4⅜"

**#8X1½" F.H.
wood screw**

Workbench Board Jack

Hold stock safely at bench
side with our quick-and-easy
adjustable support. With this
jack, you can avoid flimsy
clamping setups or having to
call a helper every time you
need to work the edge of a
long piece of stock. It also
allows you to quickly elevate
stock to a comfortable working
height. For stability, the
doweled top fits into the holes
drilled along the bottom outside
edge of the workbench shown
on *page 47.*

AIR-FILTRATION CABINET

Even with the best of dust collection systems, you can reduce airborne dust in your shop only so much. And, if you're confined to working in a small shop, or one with poor ventilation, it doesn't take much sanding or cutting to raise a cloud of fine, harmful sawdust. To help siphon off such lung-clogging dust particles, I designed and built this air-filtration cabinet.

I've made the cabinet so the top is just slightly below the top surface of our tablesaw. The cabinet top adjusts up or down if needed, enabling it to double as a handy outfeed table.

—J. R. Downing
Design Editor

Note: *We used a ¼-width blower (commonly found with heating and cooling systems) and a ¼-hp motor. See the Buying Guide on page 60 for more information or contact your local heating contractor for a used system.*

Start with the cabinet and the base

1. From ¾" plywood (for a smooth painted finish, we used birch plywood), cut the cabinet sides (A), back (B), front (C), base and top (D), support (E), and adjustable top (F) to the sizes listed in the Bill of Materials.

2. Mount a ¾" dado blade to your tablesaw, and cut ¾" rabbets ½" deep on the plywood pieces A, B, and C where shown on the Exploded View drawing and Parts View drawings. Dry-clamp the pieces (A, B, C, D, E) to check the fit.

3. Mark the switch-box hole location on one side piece (A) where shown on the Exploded View drawing. Using the Parts View drawing, mark the exhaust and handle cutouts in the back (B).

4. Drill a blade-start hole in each marked opening, and then use a

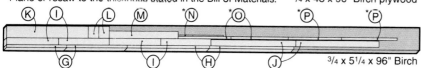

CUTTING DIAGRAM

Ⓑ　Ⓒ　Ⓓ　Ⓓ

Ⓐ　Ⓐ　Ⓕ　Ⓔ

* Plane or resaw to the thickness stated in the Bill of Materials.　　¾ x 48 x 96" Birch plywood

Ⓚ　Ⓘ　Ⓛ　Ⓜ　*Ⓝ　*Ⓞ　*Ⓟ　*Ⓟ

Ⓖ　Ⓘ　Ⓗ　Ⓙ　　¾ x 5¼ x 96" Birch

Bill of Materials

Part	Finished Size			Mat.	Qty.
	T	W	L		
BASIC CABINET					
A sides	¾"	23½"	30¼"	BP	2
B back	¾"	21"	30¼"	BP	1
C front	¾"	14"	21"	BP	1
D top & base	¾"	20½"	23½"	BP	2
E support	¾"	4¾"	19½"	BP	1
F adj. top	¾"	21"	23¾"	BP	1
G cleats	¾"	¾"	14"	B	2
H cleats	¾"	¾"	19½"	B	2
HANDLE ASSEMBLY					
I guides	¾"	1⁹⁄₁₆"	10"	B	4
J arms	¾"	1½"	19½"	B	2
FEET, CORD BAR, AND CLEATS					
K support	¾"	2½"	18"	B	1
L feet	¾"	2½"	2½"	B	2
M cord bar	¾"	1½"	16"	B	1
N cleat	¼"	¾"	10½"	B	1
O cleat	½"	¾"	13⅛"	B	2
P cleat	½"	¾"	12"	B	2

*Initially cut parts marked with an * oversized. Then, trim each to finished size according to the how-to instructions.

Material Key: BP—birch plywood, B—birch

Supplies: ½" dowel stock, 1" dowel stock, 1½X21" continuous hinge, #6X½" flathead wood screws, #8X1¼" flathead wood screws, #8X3" flathead wood screws, #10X¾" panhead screws, 2—³⁄₁₆" hanger bolts, 2—³⁄₁₆" wing nuts, 2—⅜" T-nuts, 2—⅜X1" hexhead bolts, ⅜" flat washers, ⅜" lock washers, ⅜" nuts, 4—⅜X2" hexhead bolts, #17X¾" brads, ½" hardware cloth 11X12⅝", 2—2" fixed casters, primer, paint, switch/receptacle box, 20-amp toggle switch, blank cover plate.

EXPLODED VIEW

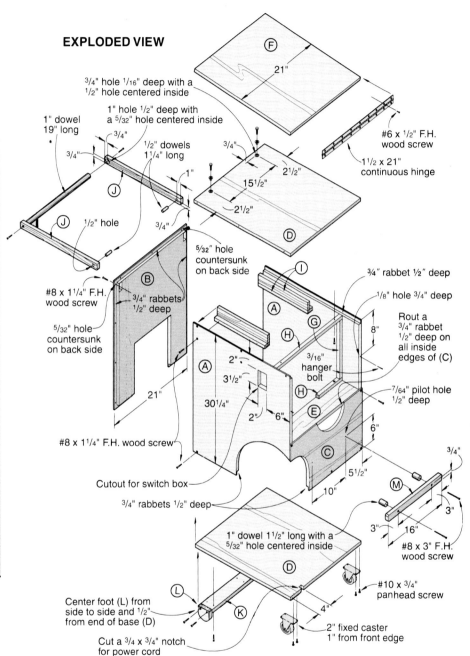

jigsaw to cut the openings to shape. Next, cut the exhaust cutout to shape.

5. Glue and clamp the cabinet assembly (A, B, C, top D, E) together. Set the base (D) aside. Check for square, and scrape off the glue squeeze-out.

6. Drill countersunk mounting holes, and reinforce the cabinet with #8X1¼" flathead wood screws where shown on the Exploded View drawing. Check the fit of the cabinet onto the base (D), and drill mounting holes for attaching the two assemblies later.

7. Cut the filter positioning cleats (G, H). Drill mounting holes, and screw the cleats in place.

Here's how to make the top adjustable

1. Drill a pair of counterbored holes in the top piece (D). (See the Exploded View drawing.)

continued

AIR-FILTRATION CABINET

continued

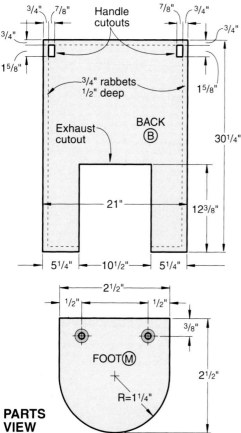

PARTS VIEW

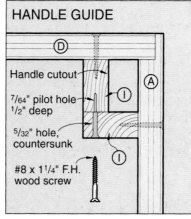

TOP ADJUSTMENT DETAIL

3/4" hole 3/8" deep centered over bolt head

TOP (F)

3/8 x 1" hexhead bolt

3/8" T-nut

(D)

HANDLE GUIDE

(D)

Handle cutout

7/64" pilot hole 1/2" deep

(A)

(I)

5/32" hole, countersunk

(I)

#8 x 1 1/4" F.H. wood screw

2. Insert a ⅜" T-nut into each hole. (To prevent the T-nuts from possibly popping loose later, we added a drop of epoxy to each hole before inserting the nut.) Thread a ⅜x1" bolt into each T-nut.

3. Cut a piece of 1½"-wide continuous hinge to 21". Drill pilot holes and fasten one leaf to the fixed cabinet top (D) and the other to the adjustable top (F).

4. Close the adjustable top (F) onto the protruding bolts in the cabinet top (D) to indent the bolt locations on the bottom of the adjustable top. Bore a pair of ¾" holes ⅜" deep on the adjustable top where indented.

Now, let's add the handle assembly

1. Cut the handle guides (I) to size. Glue and screw the guides together. (See the Exploded View and Handle Guide drawings.)

2. Hold each handle guide assembly in place inside the cabinet, and check that the handle openings align with the inside faces of the guide assemblies. Trim if necessary. Drill mounting holes, and fasten the guide assemblies to the inside of the cabinet.

3. Cut the handle arms (J) to size. Drill a 1" hole ½" deep at one end of each arm. Then, drill a ⁵⁄₃₂" shank hole centered inside the 1" hole. Drill a ½" hole 1" in from the opposite end in each arm.

4. Cut a 1" dowel to 19" long. Place the ends of the dowel in the 1" holes in the arms (J). Using previously drilled shank holes in the arms as guides, drill ⁷⁄₆₄" pilot holes 1" deep in the dowel ends.

5. With the dowel in place between the handle arms, stick the arms through the openings in the back piece (B). Slide the arms into the handle guides, and then drive

#8x1¼" screws in place to secure the arms to the 1" dowel.

6. Cut two ½" dowels to 1¼" long, and set aside for now; you'll glue them in place in the arms later.

Add the feet and cord bar

1. Cut the foot support (K) to size. Referring to the Parts View drawing, cut the feet (L) to shape.

2. Drill mounting holes and screw the feet to the support where shown on the Exploded View drawing. Screw the assembly to the bottom of the base (D).

3. Cut the cord-storage bar (M) to size. Then, cut a pair of 1" dowels to 1½" long. Drill a ⁵⁄₃₂" hole centered through each dowel. Set the pieces aside, we'll mount them to the cabinet later.

Mount the blower assembly and the electricals

1. Position the motor, blower, and bracket assembly on the base (D). Center it from side to side, and make sure that the exhaust end of the blower extends ¼" beyond the back edge of the base.

2. Using the existing holes in the blower bracket as guides, drill ⅜" holes through the base. Fasten the bracket to the base with ⅜x2" hex-head bolts where shown on the Blower Installation drawing.

3. Using the existing holes in the blower bracket as guides, drill ⁷⁄₃₂" holes into the blower housing as shown in the photo *opposite*. Fasten the blower to the metal bracket.

4. Cut the spacer cleat (N) to size, and glue and nail it in place.

5. Drill a pair of mounting holes where shown on the Exploded View drawing, and drive the ³⁄₁₆" hanger bolts into the holes. You'll use the bolts later for attaching the aluminum screen.

6. Cut two pieces of stock (we used birch) to ½x¾x30" for the hardware-cloth cleats (O, P). Cut or rout a ½" rabbet ¹⁄₁₆" deep along one edge of each cleat where shown

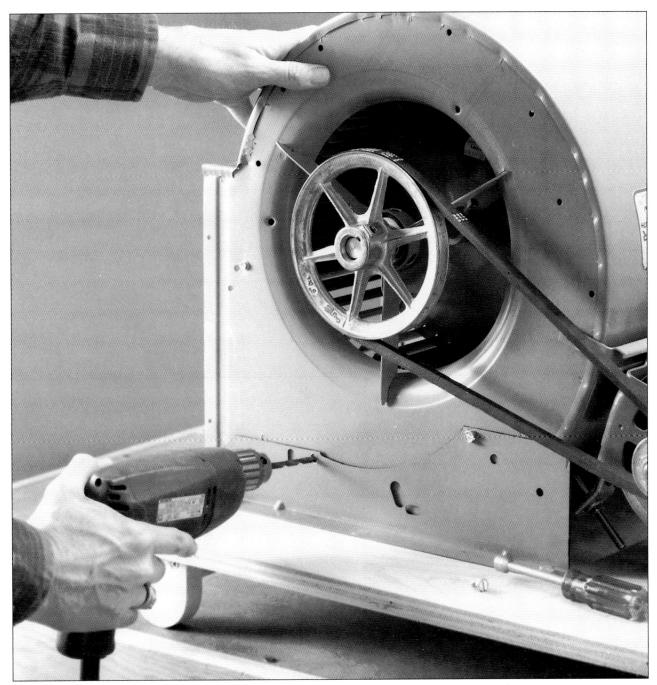

Drill holes into the blower housing, using the existing holes in the blower bracket as guides.

on the Cover detail accompanying the Blower Installation drawing. Miter-cut the four cleats to length. Drill countersunk mounting holes for attaching the cleats to the cabinet later.

Painting and final assembly

1. Fill any voids if necessary, and sand the cabinet and cleats (O, P) smooth. Remove the hardware, and prime and paint the cabinet.

2. Using a clear finish, seal the handle assembly, base and feet, and cord bar.

3. Insert the handle arms (J) through the handle openings in the back (B) and the handle guides. Working from the inside of the cabinet, glue 1¼"-long dowels into

continued

AIR-FILTRATION CABINET

continued

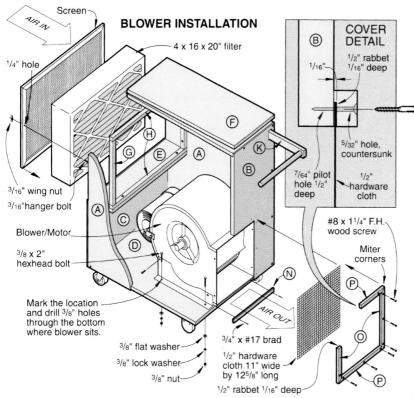

BLOWER INSTALLATION

Screen

AIR IN

4 x 16 x 20" filter

1/4" hole

3/16" wing nut

3/16"hanger bolt

Blower/Motor

3/8 x 2"
hexhead bolt

Mark the location
and drill 3/8" holes
through the bottom
where blower sits.

3/8" flat washer

3/8" lock washer

3/8" nut

AIR OUT

3/4" x #17 brad

1/2" hardware
cloth 11" wide
by 12⅝" long

1/2" rabbet 1/16" deep

**COVER
DETAIL**

1/16"

1/2" rabbet
1/16" deep

5/32" hole,
countersunk

7/64" pilot
hole 1/2"
deep

1/2"
hardware
cloth

#8 x 1¼" F.H.
wood screw

Miter
corners

base. Screw the cabinet to
the base, and add the lower
hardware cloth cleat.

Buying Guide
• **4x16x20" pleated air filter.**
For current prices, contact Iowa Air
Filter Inc., 108 SE 4th Street, Des
Moines, IA 50309, or call
800-383-5151 to order.
• **Blower and motor.** ¾-width
belt-drive blower with 10⅝"-dia-
meter wheel and ¼-hp, 1,725 rpm
motor, W.W. Grainger Stock No.
7C656. Check with your local
heating and ventilation contractor
for a new or used unit. Available
nationwide from W. W. Grainger,
Inc. Check your phone-directory
White Pages for your local branch.
Or, to mail-order the unit, call the
Des Moines, Iowa, branch of W. W.
Grainger at 515-266-3460.

the holes in the ends of the handle
arms where shown on the
Exploded View drawing.
4. Attach the cord bar where
shown on the Exploded View.
5. Cut the hardware cloth
(screen) to size, and attach it to the
cabinet with the side and top
cleats. Set the bottom cleat aside.
6. Have an aluminum-framed
screen made to cover the air intake
opening. (Our framed screen
measures 16¼x21"; we had it made
at a hardware store.) Drill a pair of
¼" holes through the screen to mate
with the ³⁄₁₆" hanger bolts in the
cabinet.
7. Screw the switch/receptacle
box to the inside of the cabinet.
Wire the toggle switch to the
motor and outlet cord as shown
right, and attach the cover plate.
Insert the filter into the opening
and fasten the framed screen in
place. Lower the cabinet onto the

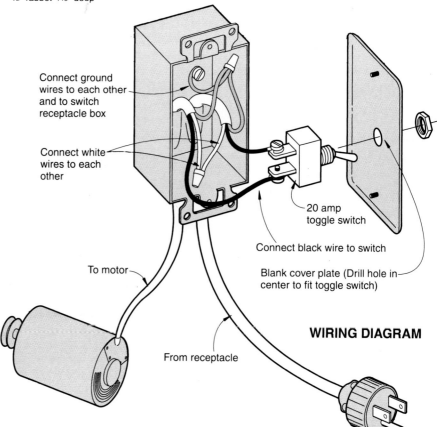

Connect ground
wires to each other
and to switch
receptacle box

Connect white
wires to each
other

20 amp
toggle switch

Connect black wire to switch

Blank cover plate (Drill hole in
center to fit toggle switch)

To motor

From receptacle

WIRING DIAGRAM

CUSTOM MITERSAW CABINET

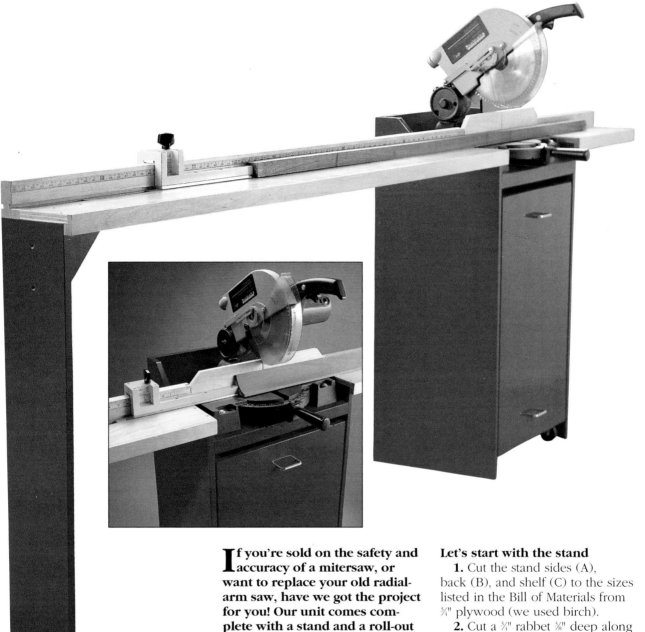

If you're sold on the safety and accuracy of a mitersaw, or want to replace your old radial-arm saw, have we got the project for you! Our unit comes complete with a stand and a roll-out bin for chips and cut-offs. Add to that an extended fence and its hairline-accurate stop, and you've put your miter- and cross-cutting problems to an end.

Note: We designed this cabinet to support a DeWalt 8½" mitersaw measuring 18" wide by 20" deep. You may need to change some dimensions to fit your mitersaw.

Let's start with the stand

1. Cut the stand sides (A), back (B), and shelf (C) to the sizes listed in the Bill of Materials from ¾" plywood (we used birch).

2. Cut a ⅜" rabbet ⅜" deep along the back inside edge of each cabinet side (A) where shown on the Stand and Mobile Bin drawing on *page 62.*

3. Using the dimensions on the drawing, mark the angled layout on the top end of the side pieces, and cut the ends to shape.

4. Cut the shelf banding strip (D) to size, and then cut or rout a ¾"
continued

CUSTOM MITERSAW CABINET
continued

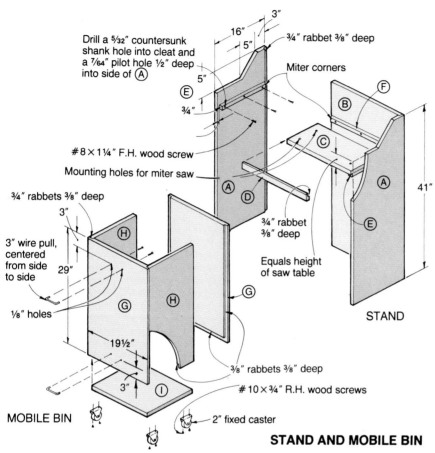

Drill a 5/32" countersunk shank hole into cleat and a 7/64" pilot hole 1/2" deep into side of (A)

3/4" rabbet 3/8" deep

Miter corners

#8 × 1¼" F.H. wood screw

Mounting holes for miter saw

3/4" rabbets 3/8" deep

3" wire pull, centered from side to side

1/8" holes

3/4" rabbet 3/8" deep

Equals height of saw table

STAND

3/8" rabbets 3/8" deep

#10 × 3/4" R.H. wood screws

2" fixed caster

MOBILE BIN

STAND AND MOBILE BIN

Bill of Materials					
Part	**Finished Size**			**Mat.**	**Qty.**
	T	**W**	**L**		
STAND					
A sides	¾"	16"	41"	BP	2
B back	¾"	20¾"	41"	BP	1
C shelf	¾"	8¾"	20"	BP	1
D band	¾"	1½"	20"	B	1
E shelf supports	¾"	1"	14½"	B	2
F dust strip	¾"	1"	20"	B	1
MOBILE BIN					
G front & back	¾"	19½"	29"	BP	2
H sides	¾"	14¼"	29"	BP	2
I bottom	¾"	14¼"	18¾"	BP	1
TABLES AND FENCES					
J table	¾"	4⅝"	75"	BP	1
K table	¾"	5⅜"	18"	BP	1
L band	¾"	1½"	75"	B	1
M band	¾"	1½"	18"	B	1
N spacers	¾"	¾"	1"	B	10
O fence	1¹⁄₁₆"	2¾"	75"	B	1
P fence	1¹⁄₁₆"	2¾"	18"	B	1
Q fence	½"	3"	21"	B	1
R support	¾"	4¼"	35¼"	BP	1
S braces	¾"	10"	10"	BP	2
SUPPORT BRACKET					
T support arm	¾"	2"	13⅜"	B	1
U cleat	¾"	1"	2"	B	1

Material Key: BP—birch plywood, B—birch

Supplies: #8X1¼" flathead wood screws, #8X1½" flathead wood screws, #8X2" flathead wood screws, #8X3" flathead wood screws, #10X2½" flathead wood screws, 4—2" fixed casters with #10X¾" roundhead wood screws for mounting, 2—¼" threaded inserts, 2—¼" nuts, 2—adjustable nylon floor glides, 2—3" metal wire pulls, adhesive-backed tape measure, enamel paint.

rabbet ⅜" deep along the top inside edge. Glue and clamp the strip to the front edge of the shelf (C) with the ends and top surfaces flush.

5. Cut the two shelf supports (E) and rear dust-deflector strip (F) to size.

Note: *Position the fixed shelf (C) so the table of your mitersaw is flush with the top surface of the extension tables (J, K). Depending on your particular mitersaw, your shelf height may be different from ours.*

6. Measure and mark the locations for the shelf supports and dust strip where shown on the Stand and Mobile Bin drawing *above.* Then, drill and countersink mounting holes through the stand assembly, and screw the shelf supports and dust strip to the stand.

7. Glue and clamp the stand together, checking for square.

It's time to roll out the mobile bin

1. Cut the bin front and back (G), sides (H), and bottom (I) to size (we used birch plywood).

2. Cut rabbets along the front, back, and side pieces to the sizes given on the Stand and Mobile Bin drawing.

3. Glue and clamp the bin together, checking for square. Later, remove the clamps, drill mounting holes, and mount four 2" fixed casters to the bottom of the bin. Drill the holes for a pair of 3" wire pulls in the bin front. The bottom pull makes for ease in lifting when discarding the contents.

Let's make the extension table and fence assemblies

1. Cut the left-hand tabletop extension (J), right-hand tabletop extension (K), banding strips

(L, M), and spacers (N) to size. The spacers allow chips and sawdust to fall through the extension tables, avoiding buildup against the fence and stop.

2. Cut the fences (O, P, Q) to size. For smooth sliding of the stop on part O later, ensure that part O is uniform in thickness and width.

3. Cut a ¹⁷⁄₃₂" groove ¹⁄₁₆" deep along the front face of part O to house the tape measure.

4. Using the Top View detail accompanying the Exploded View drawing for reference, cut a ¼" slot ½" deep across one end of parts O and P. Then, cut a ½" rabbet ¼" deep across both ends of the middle replaceable fence (Q) to form a tongue that will mate in the outside-fence slots.

5. Cut a pair of ⁵⁄₁₆" grooves ¼" deep along the front and back of the left-hand fence (O) where shown on the End View detail.

6. Glue and screw the spacers (N) between the left-hand fence (O) and table (J) with the top surface of the table flush with those of the spacers. Glue and clamp the banding strips (L, M) to the front of their respective tables.

7. Cut the left-hand fence assembly support (R) and braces

(S) to size. Drill the mounting holes and screw a pair of ¼" T-nuts into the mounting holes in the bottom of the support (R) to the sizes shown on the Foot detail accompanying the Exploded View drawing *below*.

8. Glue and screw the right-hand fence (P) and brace (S) to the table (K). Then, as shown in the photo on the opposite page, screw the table (K) and brace (S) to the right-hand stand side (A). (We used a square-cut corner support (R) to hold the table assembly square when attaching it to the stand.)

9. Drill the mounting holes, and glue and screw the support (R) and brace (S) to the left-hand table assembly.

Anchor the long extension table to the wall

1. Position the stand with its back edge flush with a wall in your workshop. Position your mitersaw on the stand. Verify that the top surface of the saw table is flush with the right- and left-hand extension tables. Adjust the shelf height if necessary.

continued

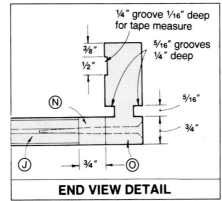

END VIEW DETAIL

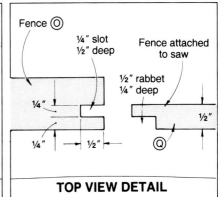

TOP VIEW DETAIL

EXPLODED VIEW

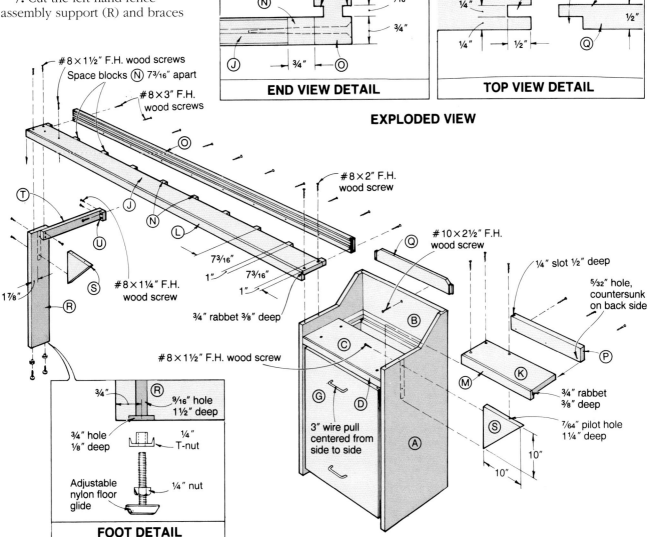

FOOT DETAIL

CUSTOM MITERSAW CABINET
continued

Bill of Materials

Part	Finished size			Mat.	Qty.
	T	W	L		
STOP BLOCK					
A top	¾"	2⅝"	3"	BP	1
B posts	¾"	¾"	1¼"	BP	2
C back	¾"	2"	3"	BP	1
D* extension	¾"	¾"	13¾"	B	1

*Initial size before cutting to length.

Material Key: BP—birch plywood, B—birch
Supplies: epoxy, #6X⅜" roundhead brass wood screws, #6X⅝" flathead wood screw, ¼" all-thread rod 1½" long, ¼" T-nuts, #10X1" flathead machine screws, #10X3 " flathead machine screws, ⅛X1¼X1⅞" acrylic, ¼X1X20" aluminum bar stock.

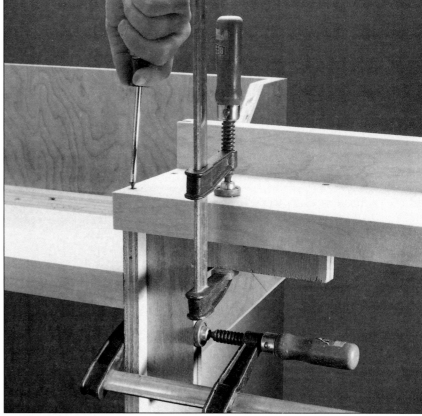

Fasten the table and brace to the bin side, using a square-cut corner support for stability.

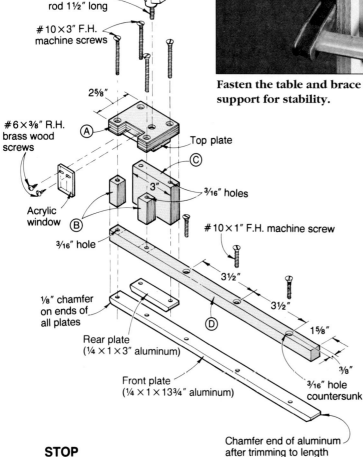

Knob

¼" all-thread rod 1½" long

#10×3" F.H. machine screws

2⅝"

#6×⅜" R.H. brass wood screws

(A)

Top plate

(C)

3"   ³⁄₁₆" holes

Acrylic window

(B)

³⁄₁₆" hole

#10×1" F.H. machine screw

⅛" chamfer on ends of all plates

Rear plate (¼ × 1 × 3" aluminum)

3½"

3½"

(D)

1⅝"

⅜"

³⁄₁₆" hole countersunk

Front plate (¼ × 1 × 13¾" aluminum)

Chamfer end of aluminum after trimming to length

STOP

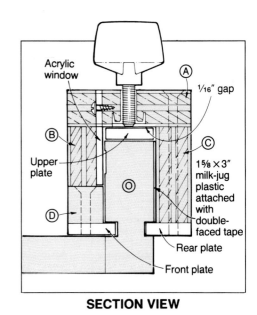

Acrylic window

(A)

¹⁄₁₆" gap

(B)

Upper plate

(C)

1⅝ × 3" milk-jug plastic attached with double-faced tape

(D)

(O)

Rear plate

Front plate

SECTION VIEW

2. Fasten the left-hand fence to the stand, and adjust the floor glides in the end support (R). Use a straight-edge or long straight board to check that the left-hand tabletop (J) aligns with right-hand tabletop (K).

3. Cut the support arm (T) and cleat (U) to size.

4. Sand, prime, and paint the stand, bin, and table support (see the opening photo for specifics). We used red aerosol enamel.

5. Attach the support arm and cleat to the end support (R). Screw cleat to your shop wall to brace the end of the left-hand extension table against the wall.

6. Drill a mounting hole in the stand back (B) where shown on the Exploded View drawing, allowing you to anchor the stand firmly to the wall.

For consistent lengths, add the stop block

1. Cut the stop top (A), posts (B), back (C), and extension (D) to sizes listed in the Bill of Materials.

2. Using the Stop and Parts View drawings for locations, epoxy the parts together where shown. After the epoxy has cured, drill and countersink all holes through the assembly where dimensioned on the drawing *page 66* for reference. Don't forget to drill the counter-bored hole on the bottom.

3. From ¼x1" aluminum, cut the top, front, and rear plates to length (we used a hacksaw).

4. Clamp or tape the aluminum strips to the stop assembly where shown on the Section View detail accompanying the Stop drawing. Using the existing holes in the stop as guides, drill ⁵⁄₃₂" holes through the aluminum. Using a 10–24 tap, thread the holes in the front and rear plate to mate with #10 machine screws.

5. Drill and countersink a ⁵⁄₃₂" hole in the aluminum Top Plate where shown on the Stop Top drawing.

6. Epoxy a ¼" T-nut into the counterbored hole on the bottom side of part A. Be careful not to get epoxy in the threaded opening of the T-nut.

7. From ⅛" acrylic, cut the window to the size shown on the Parts View drawing. Drill holes side by side to form a pair of adjustment slots. Scribe a line down the center of the window. Highlight the line with a black marker.

8. Sand a chamfer on each end of the aluminum top plate where shown on the Stop Top drawing.

Assemble the stop pieces

1. Screw the three aluminum plates to the stop assembly.

2. Cut a piece of ¼" all-thread rod to 1½" long. Epoxy and thread one end into the knob. Sand or grind a slight chamfer onto the bottom end of the threaded rod.

3. Fasten the top plate to the stop top where shown on the Stop Top drawing. Back the screw out slightly to create a ¹⁄₁₆" gap between the end of the plate and the stop top (A) where shown on the Section View drawing accompanying the Stop drawing.

4. Mask the aluminum, and paint the stop. Fasten the acrylic window
continued

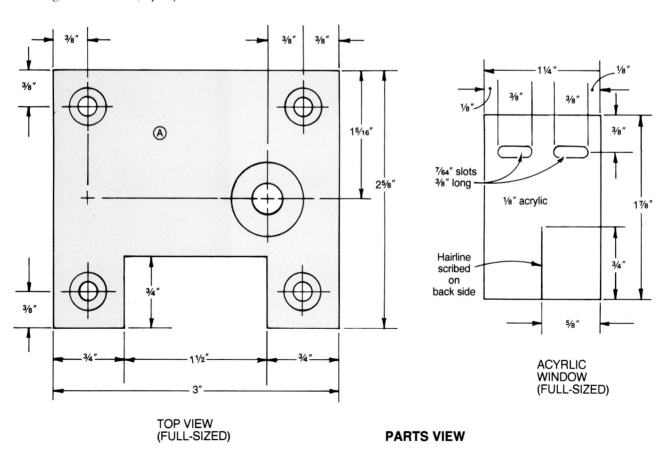

TOP VIEW
(FULL-SIZED)

PARTS VIEW

ACYRLIC
WINDOW
(FULL-SIZED)

CUSTOM MITERSAW CABINET
continued

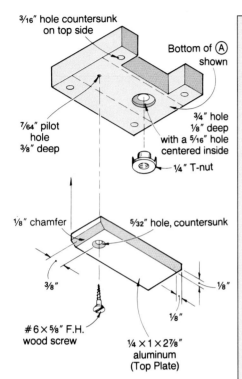

3/16" hole countersunk on top side

Bottom of (A) shown

7/64" pilot hole 3/8" deep

3/4" hole 1/8" deep with a 5/16" hole centered inside

1/4" T-nut

1/8" chamfer

5/32" hole, countersunk

3/8"

1/8"

1/8"

#6×5/8" F.H. wood screw

1/4×1×2 7/8" aluminum (Top Plate)

STOP TOP

to the stop so the screws are centered in the adjustment slots.

5. Cut a piece of milk-jug plastic to 1⅜×3". Using double-faced cloth-backed tape, adhere the plastic to part C where shown in the Section View detail. The plastic helps the stop slide smoothly.

Buying Guide
• **Mitersaw cabinet hardware kit.** 72" adhesive-backed tape measure, knob, ¼" threaded rod 1½" long, ¼×1×24" aluminum (holes are not drilled or tapped), ⅛×1¼×1⅞" acrylic, 4—#10×3" F.H. machine screws, 3—#10×1" F.H. machine screws, 2—6×⅜" roundhead brass wood screws, #6×⅝" F.H. wood screw, 3—¼" T-nuts, 2—adjustable nylon floor glides. Kit No. MS2273. For current prices, contact Puckett Electric, 841 11th St., Des Moines, IA 50309, or call 800-544-4189 or 515-244-4189 to order.

Get ready...get set...cut

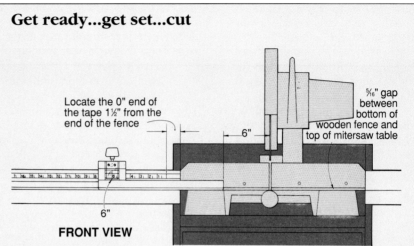

Locate the 0" end of the tape 1½" from the end of the fence

6"

6"

5/16" gap between bottom of wooden fence and top of mitersaw table

FRONT VIEW

Set your mitersaw on the shelf (C) and check that the top surface of the saw table is flush with the top surfaces of the extension tables (K, L). Slide the middle fence (Q) in position, leaving a 5/16" gap between the bottom edge of the fence and the top edge of the mitersaw table. See the Front View drawing for reference.

Position the mitersaw so the mitersaw fence is directly behind the middle fence (Q). Trace the location of the mounting holes in the mitersaw fence onto the middle fence (C). Drill mounting holes, and then fasten the middle fence to the mitersaw fence.

Drill mounting holes, and bolt the saw to the shelf. Attach the adhesive-backed tape measure to the left-hand fence where shown on the drawing *above*. For easier sliding, rub paraffin on the mating parts of the stop and fence.

Slide the stop assembly onto the fence so the aluminum front and rear plates slide freely in the grooves in the left-hand extension fence. Position the stop so the marked hairline on the acrylic window centers over the beginning (0") on the tape. Tighten the knob to lock the stop on the fence. Using a fine-toothed carbide-tipped blade, cut the end of the stop extension to length.

Now, by moving the stop exactly 6" away from the blade, the hairline marked on the acrylic window will automatically align over the 6" marking on the tape. Should you ever need to adjust the window, loosen the #6 screws slightly, adjust as necessary, and tighten the screws. Remove the stop, and sand or file a slight chamfer on the cut end of the front aluminum plate.

CUSTOMIZED TABLESAW BASE

Here's a great-looking addition for your shop, with lots of advantages over run-of-the-mill tablesaw stands. The thing I think you'll appreciate most about this project is the dust-gathering performance made possible by the enclosed top compartment. But that's not the only goodie I've designed into the base. You'll also find nifty places to store your pushstick, miter gauge, rip fence, saws blades, and a wrench to change those blades. The whole project, including the hardware, costs less than $75.

—J. R. Downing
Design Editor

Note: We sized our base to fit a Sears 10" direct-drive tablesaw. The sides of the base are flush with the sides of the saw. You may have to alter the base size to fit your particular saw.

Construction begins with the cabinet carcass

1. Rip and crosscut the two side panels (A), dividers (B), and back (C) to the sizes listed in the Bill of Materials from ¾" particleboard.

2. Cut or rout ¾" dadoes ¼" deep in each side panel for the dividers to fit into. See the Exploded View drawing on *page 68* for location. Cut a ¾" rabbet ¼" deep along the back edge of each side panel.

3. Measure the outside diameter of your vacuum hose (we measured ours at 2½" with an outside calipers). Using a compass, center and mark the hole location to the back (C) where shown on the Exploded View drawing. Drill a blade-start hole, and cut the hole to size with a circle cutter or jigsaw.

4. Glue and clamp the dividers and back piece between the side panels, checking for square. After the glue dries, remove the clamps, and sand the joints. Rout a ¼" round-over along the edges of the base where shown on the Exploded View drawing.

For safe cutting later, make a pushstick

1. Cut a piece of heavy paper to 4×13", and draw a 1" grid on it. Using the grid pattern *below* for reference, lay out the pushstick shape on the gridded paper. To do this, mark the points where the pattern outline crosses each grid line. Next, draw lines to connect the points. Mark the centerpoints for the two ¾" holes.

2. Cut the paper pattern to shape, and use it as a template to transfer the full-sized pushstick pattern to ½" plywood. Cut the pushstick to shape. Bore two ¾" holes through the pushstick where marked.

3. Add two nails to the access panel for holding the pushstick.

Attach the trim, and mount the cleats and access panel

1. Cut the baseboard parts (D, E) to size plus 2" in length. (We chose birch; you also could use good-quality 2x6 material.) Bevel-rip a 1¼" chamfer along the top outside
continued

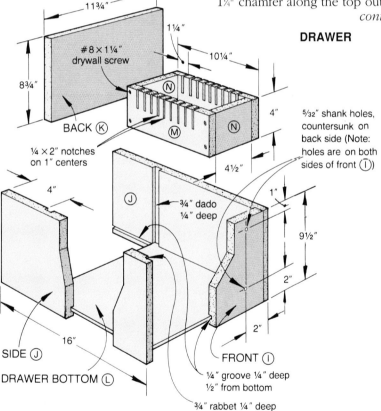

DRAWER

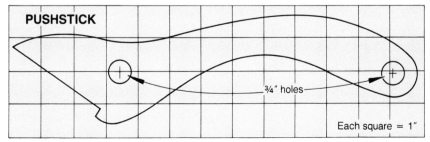

PUSHSTICK

¾" holes

Each square = 1"

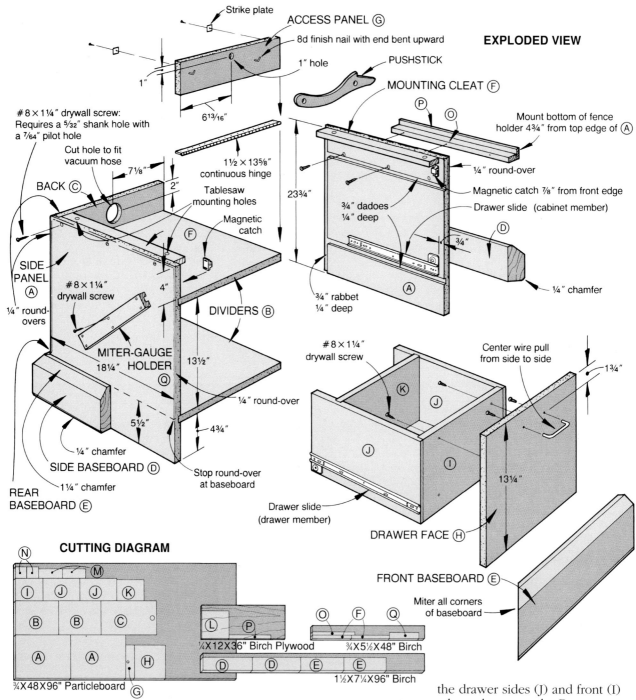

EXPLODED VIEW

Strike plate

ACCESS PANEL G

8d finish nail with end bent upward

1" hole

PUSHSTICK

MOUNTING CLEAT F

Mount bottom of fence holder 4¾" from top edge of (A)

¼" round-over

Magnetic catch ⅞" from front edge

Drawer slide (cabinet member)

¾" dadoes ¼" deep

¾" rabbet ¼" deep

23¾"

¼" chamfer

#8 × 1¼" drywall screw: Requires a 5/32" shank hole with a 7/64" pilot hole

Cut hole to fit vacuum hose

7⅛"

2"

1½ × 13⅝" continuous hinge

6¹³⁄₁₆"

Tablesaw mounting holes

Magnetic catch

BACK C

SIDE PANEL A

¼" round-overs

#8 × 1¼" drywall screw

MITER-GAUGE HOLDER Q

18¼"

DIVIDERS B

13½"

4"

¼" round-over

5½"

4¾"

Center wire pull from side to side

1¾"

#8 × 1¼" drywall screw

13¼"

¼" chamfer

SIDE BASEBOARD D

1¼" chamfer

Stop round-over at baseboard

REAR BASEBOARD E

Drawer slide (drawer member)

DRAWER FACE H

FRONT BASEBOARD E

Miter all corners of baseboard

CUTTING DIAGRAM

N
M
I J J K
B B C
A A H
¾"X48X96" Particleboard G

L P
¼X12X36" Birch Plywood

O F Q
¾X5½X48" Birch

D D E E
1½X7¼X96" Birch

edge and a ¼" chamfer along the bottom outside edge of each piece. Miter-cut the pieces to length, and glue and clamp them flush with the bottom of the cabinet.

2. Cut the mounting cleats (F) to size, drill mounting holes through the side panels, and screw the cleats flush with the top edge of the cabinet sides where shown on the Exploded View drawing.

3. Cut the access panel (G) to size. Mark the location, and bore a 1" finger hole in the access panel.

Add the drawer and blade rack

1. From ¾" particleboard, cut the drawer face (H), front (I), sides (J), and back (K) to the sizes listed in the Bill of Materials. Cut the drawer bottom (L) to size.

2. Cut or rout a ¼" groove ¼" deep ½" from the bottom edge into

the drawer sides (J) and front (I) where shown on the Drawer drawing on *page 67*. Now, cut a ¾" dado ¼" deep 4" from the back edge in each drawer side. Next, cut or rout a ¾" rabbet ¼" deep along the front edge of each side. Dry-clamp the pieces to check the fit.

3. Glue and clamp together the drawer (I, J, K, L), checking for square. Using the Drawer drawing for reference, mark the center-points, and drill four shank holes through the front (I). Countersink

Bill of Materials

Parts	Finished Size			Mat.	Qty.
	T	W	L		
BASE CABINET					
A sides	¾"	18¼"	23¾"	PB	2
B dividers	¾"	14¼"	17½"	PB	2
C back	¾"	14¼"	23¾"	PB	1
D* side basebrd	1½"	5½"	21¼"	B	2
E* frt & bk basebrd	1½"	5½"	18¼"	B	2
F cleat	¾"	1¾"	16¾"	B	2
G panel	¾"	3¾"	13⅜"	PB	1
DRAWER					
H face	¾"	13¼"	13½"	PB	1
I front	¾"	9½"	11¾"	PB	1
J sides	¾"	9½"	16 "	PB	2
K back	¾"	8¾"	11¾"	PB	1
L bottom	¼"	11½"	11¾"	P	1
M sides	¾"	4"	10¼"	PB	2
N bottom	¾"	4"	4½"	PB	2
FENCE AND MITER-GAUGE HOLDERS					
O bottom	¾"	1½"	17½"	B	1
P side	¼"	1½"	17½"	P	1
Q holder	¾"	2½"	12½"	B	1

*Initially cut parts marked with an * oversized. Then, trim them to finished size according to the how-to instructions.

Material Key: PB—particleboard, B—birch, P—plywood

Supplies: #8X1¼" drywall screws, two magnetic catches, 8d finish nails, 1½X13⅜" continuous hinge, 3" wire pull (handle), set of drawer slides (we used Knape & Vogt 16" drawer slide 1300), wood putty, sanding sealer, enamel paint.

MITER-GAUGE HOLDER

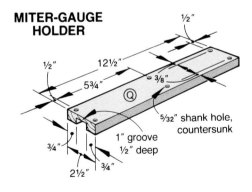

½"
½"
12½"
5¾"
⅜"
Q
5/32" shank hole, countersunk
1" groove ½" deep
¾"
¾"
2½"

the holes on the back side of the drawer front. You'll use these holes later for attaching the drawer face.

4. Cut the blade rack parts (M, N) to size and cut the dadoes where shown in the drawing on *page 67.* Assemble the rack.

Let's add the fence and miter-gauge holders

1. Cut the fence holder parts (O, P) to size. Glue and clamp O to P, with the bottom edges and ends flush. Glue and screw the fence holder to the right-hand side panel (A) where shown on the Exploded View drawing.

2. Cut a piece of ¾"-thick birch to 2½" wide by 12½" long for the miter-gauge holder (Q). Cut or rout a 1" groove ½" deep along the center of part Q. See the Miter Gauge Holder drawing for location.

3. Drill six 5/32" shank holes through the holder (Q) where shown on the Miter-Gauge Holder drawing. Set it aside; you'll attach it later.

Mount the access panel, magnetic catches, and pull

1. Cut one piece of ¾" continuous hinge to 13⅝" long. Screw the hinge to the bottom edge of the access panel (G) and to the top of the upper divider (B) so the access panel closes flush with the front of the divider and the side panels.

2. Fasten the magnetic catches to the side panel (A) ⅞" from the front edge. Now, close the access door and mark the mating location on the back side of the door for the strike plates. Fasten the strike plates to the back side of the access door.

3. Locate and drill the wire-pull holes through the drawer face. Attach the wire pull.

Mount the drawer slides and drawer face

1. Position the front edge of one of the drawer slides flush with the front edge of one of the drawer sides (J). Position the back bottom edge of the roller flush with the bottom edge of the drawer side. Fasten the roller end of the slide to the drawer side.

2. As shown in the photo *top right,* use a combination square to keep the slide parallel with the bottom edge of the drawer, and fasten the slide to the drawer side. Repeat the procedure to fasten the other slide.

3. Fasten the mating slide components to the sides (A), with the bottom edge of the slide flush

Position the drawer slide parallel to the bottom of the drawer.

with the top surface of the divider and ¾" back from the cabinet front.

4. Slide the drawer into the cabinet and adjust the slides if necessary.

Center the drawer face in the opening, and adhere it to the drawer.

Place several large pieces of double-faced tape on the front face of the drawer front (I). Using ⅛" spacers, center the drawer face (H) over the drawer in the opening as shown in the photo *above left.* Now, press firmly against the drawer face to adhere it to the drawer front

5. Remove the drawer assembly from the cabinet. Fasten the drawer face to the drawer front with four #8X1¼" drywall screws using the holes previously drilled in the drawer front.

Apply the finish

1. Position your tablesaw (minus the metal base) over your new base. Trace the location of the mounting holes from the tablesaw to the cleats. With the saw still resting on the base, position the miter-gauge holder, and glue and screw it to the left-hand side panel (A).

2. Remove the saw from the base and drill the mounting holes

3. Mask the continuous hinge, and remove the rest of the hardware from the cabinet. Finish-sand the base and drawer. Fill all exposed edges with putty and sand smooth.

4. Apply one coat of sanding sealer to the base. Let dry, and hand-sand smooth. Repeat this process twice.

5. Spray several coats (we applied three) of an enamel paint to the base. (We took a piece of metal from our tablesaw to a paint store, and had them mix paint to match.) Fasten the tablesaw to the base.

ROUTER EXTENSION TABLE

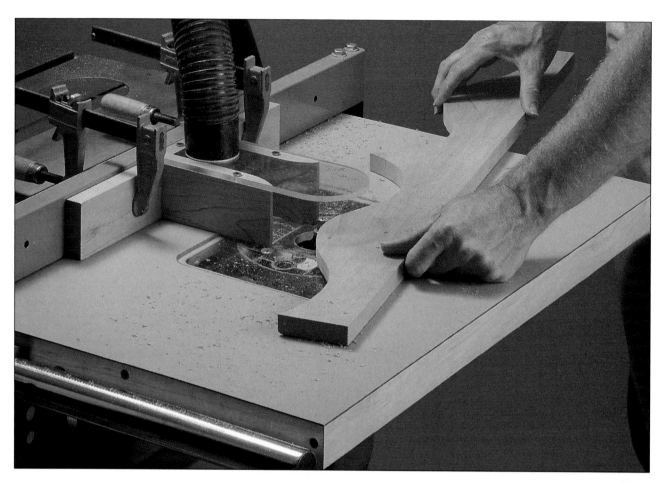

If you haven't already done so, you really owe it to yourself to add a router-table extension like this to your tablesaw. It's easy. Just remove the right-hand metal extension that's on your saw now, and then build and bolt this one in place. The extension allows you to make good use of already-available space, and it puts your router at a comfortable height.

Note: We made our extension table to fit a Delta 10" contractor's saw. Dimensions and connection assembly may vary for your saw. For other tablesaws, we recommend making the tabletop as wide as the extension being replaced and as long as the front and rear rails can sturdily support. Often, the extension table can be longer than the metal extension it's replacing.

Construct the tabletop assembly first

1. Cut the extension tabletop (A) to size from ¾" plywood (we used birch plywood).

2. Cut the banding strips (B, C) to size, mitering the ends.

3. To mount the banding strips to the plywood, drill and countersink mounting holes through the strips and into the tabletop edges. With the top edges flush, glue and screw the strips to the tabletop. Sand the top surface of the banding flush with the top of the plywood tabletop.

4. Measure the length and width of the banded top, and cut a piece of plastic laminate to the measured size plus 1" in length and width. Using contact cement, center and adhere the plastic laminate to the top of the tabletop assembly (A, B, C).

5. Fit your router with a flush-trimming bit, and rout the edges of the laminate flush with the edges of the banding.

6. Follow Steps 1 through 5 on the Tabletop Layout drawing *opposite* to form the opening in the tabletop for the router plate. (When routing the ⅜" rabbet ⅜" deep in step 5 of the drawing, we routed to ⁵⁄₁₆" deep on the first pass, and then routed ¼" deeper per pass until the top surface of the plate was perfectly flush with the top surface of the tabletop laminate. See the Buying Guide for our source of a precut router plate. Or have a piece of ⅜" acrylic cut to size.)

Now, mount the extension to the saw table

1. Follow the four-step drawing *opposite, bottom* to mark and drill

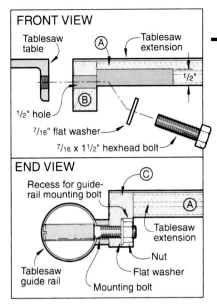

FRONT VIEW

Tablesaw table
Tablesaw extension
Ⓐ
1/2"
Ⓑ
1/2" hole
7/16" flat washer
7/16 x 1 1/2" hexhead bolt

END VIEW

Recess for guide-rail mounting bolt
Ⓒ
Ⓐ
Tablesaw extension
Nut
Flat washer
Tablesaw guide rail
Mounting bolt

MOUNTING THE EXTENSION

Bill of Materials

Part	Finished Size			Mat.	Qty.
	T	W	L		
A tabletop	3/4"	15 1/2"	25 1/2"	BP	1
B banding	3/4"	1 1/2"	27"	M	2
C banding	3/4"	1 1/2"	17"	M	2

Material Key: BP–birch plywood, M–maple.

Supplies: #8X1 1/4" flathead wood screws, 18X28" plastic laminate, contact cement, bolts and flat washers for mounting the extension table to saw table.

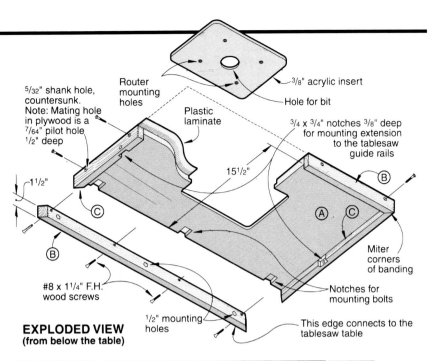

5/32" shank hole, countersunk. Note: Mating hole in plywood is a 7/64" pilot hole 1/2" deep

Router mounting holes

Plastic laminate

3/8" acrylic insert
Hole for bit

3/4 x 3/4" notches 3/8" deep for mounting extension to the tablesaw guide rails

15 1/2"

1 1/2"

Ⓒ

Ⓑ

Ⓐ Ⓒ

Miter corners of banding

Ⓑ

#8 x 1 1/4" F.H. wood screws

1/2" mounting holes

Notches for mounting bolts

This edge connects to the tablesaw table

EXPLODED VIEW
(from below the table)

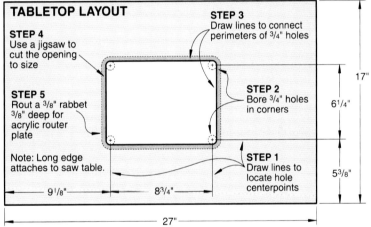

TABLETOP LAYOUT

STEP 4
Use a jigsaw to cut the opening to size

STEP 5
Rout a 3/8" rabbet 3/8" deep for acrylic router plate

Note: Long edge attaches to saw table.

STEP 3
Draw lines to connect perimeters of 3/4" holes

STEP 2
Bore 3/4" holes in corners

STEP 1
Draw lines to locate hole centerpoints

17"

6 1/4"

5 3/8"

9 1/8"

8 3/4"

27"

the mounting holes in the tablesaw extension. Before drilling, double-check that the top surface of the extension table will be perfectly flush with the top surface of your saw table.

2. Use a chisel to form 1 1/2"-wide by 1 3/4"-long by 1/2"-deep notches on the bottom side of the extension for housing the hexhead bolts. See the Front View drawing *above* for reference. Fasten the extension to the saw table.

3. Using the holes in the guide rails as guides, mark their location onto the outside surfaces of both banding pieces (C). Remove the extension table from the saw table, and drill the guide-rail mounting holes where marked. See the End View for reference. Chisel a 3/8"-deep notch on the inside face of the banding strips (the mounting bolts aren't long enough to go completely through the 3/4"-thick banding).

4. With the top edges perfectly flush, fasten the extension table to the saw table and rails.

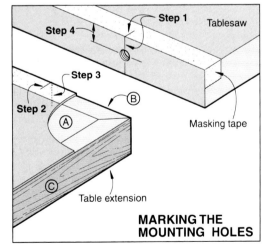

Step 1
Tablesaw
Step 4
Step 3
Ⓑ
Step 2
Ⓐ
Ⓒ
Masking tape
Table extension

MARKING THE MOUNTING HOLES

Step 1. Mark and transfer the centerlines from the saw-table holes to masking tape.
Step 2. Position the extension table against the saw table, and transfer the marks.
Step 3. With a square, extend the lines down the edge of the table extension banding (B).
Step 4. Measure the distance from the top of the saw table to the centerline of the existing hole. Transfer that dimension to the table extension. Drill the mounting holes through the banding.

Buying Guide
• **Router plate.** 3/8x7 3/4x10 1/4" clear acrylic insert. Catalog No. 101. If your router uses metric screws, specify router brand and model for a set of extra-long screws for mounting the router to the plate. For current prices, contact Woodhaven, 5323 W. Kimberly Rd., Davenport, IA 52806, or call 800-344-6657 or 319-391-2386.

THE ULTIMATE ROUTER FENCE SYSTEM

With space at a premium in my shop, I need everything to work doubly hard. With that in mind, I decided to mount my router under a tablesaw extension (shown on *page 70*), enabling me to clamp the router fence to my standard tablesaw fence. I designed the router fence with a pickup for dust collection, a high fence for vertical stability, and a right-angle support for biscuit joinery. A clear acrylic guard helps ensure safety and an acrylic plate in the center allows me to see the bit. I also added a pushblock to minimize chip-out and ensure safety when cutting end grain.

— J. R. Downing
Design Editor

Prepare the pieces for the fence assembly

1. From ¾" plywood (we used birch), cut the upright (A), base (B), clamping fence (C), and fence supports (D) to the sizes listed in the Bill of Materials.

2. Transfer the dimensions from the Parts View drawing to the supports (D); cut them to shape.

3. Mark the hole centerpoint on one support for a vacuum-hose opening. Clamp the support to your drill-press table, and bore a hole in the support to accommodate your vacuum hose. (We used a circle cutter to cut a 2¼" hole to fit our particular shop vac hose.) You could also drill a blade-start hole, and cut the vacuum hole to shape with a scrollsaw or jigsaw.

4. Using the Fence drawing for reference, mark the centerpoints, and drill all the mounting holes in the upright (A). Don't forget to drill three ¾" counterbores ⅛" deep with a ⁵⁄₁₆" hole centered inside for the ¼" T-nuts.

5. Mark the location, and cut the 1¾x2" notch in the upright (A) and a ¾x2" notch in B. Next, cut a ¹⁄₁₆x¹⁄₁₆" sawdust kerf along the bottom front edge of the upright.

6. Tap three ¼" T-nuts into their mating counterbored holes in the back surface of the upright (A).

7. Drill a 2" hole in the base for hanging when not in use.

Assemble the fence assembly

1. Clamp the upright to the base, and use the previously drilled mounting holes in the upright to drill the pilot holes centered along the front edge of the base.

2. Glue and screw the upright to the base. Before the glue dries, glue and screw the supports (D) in place to keep the upright square to the base.

3. Tilt your tablesaw blade 2° from vertical, and raise it 2½" above the surface of the saw table. Bevel-cut the *back edge* of the base and supports. Bevel-cutting this edge at 2° ensures that the clamping fence (C) is positioned 2° from vertical after it is attached to base/supports. When clamping the assembled fence to your tablesaw fence later, the bevel causes the front edge of the fence to be held firmly against the router-table surface. This prevents sawdust and chips from building up between the fence and table.

4. Drill the mounting holes, and glue and screw the clamping fence (C) to the back beveled edge of the fence assembly.

5. From ¼" acrylic, cut the dust cover to size, bevel-cutting or sanding the ends at a 25° angle where shown on the Parts View.

6. Drill and countersink mounting holes through the acrylic dust cover and into the top edge of each support (D).

Let's construct the pushblock

1. Cut the pushblock handle (E), base (F), and removable fence (G) to the sizes listed in the Bill of Materials.

2. Enlarge and transfer the gridded patterns (E, F) from the Parts View drawing to the stock. Clamp the handle blank (E) in a handscrew clamp for support, and use a brad-point bit and your drill press to drill a ½" hole 2" deep in the bottom of the handle blank.

3. Cut the pieces to shape and sand smooth. Rout ¼" round-overs along the edges of the handle where shown on the Pushblock drawing.

4. Bore a ½" and ¾" hole in the base where shown on the Parts View *opposite center*.

5. Cut a ½" dowel to 2¾" long. Glue and dowel the pushblock handle (E) to the base (F). Then, drill the mounting holes, and screw (no glue) the fence (G) to the base. The fence piece is not glued in place, making it easier to replace later, after you've routed into it numerous times.

Now, let's build the right-angle support

1. Cut the mounting plate (H) and support piece (I) to shape. See

continued

Bill of Materials					
Part	**Finished Size**			**Mat.**	**Qty.**
	T	**W**	**L**		
FENCE ASSEMBLY					
A upright	¾"	5"	27"	BP	1
B base	¾"	5½"	27"	BP	1
C clamping fence	¾"	2½"	27"	BP	1
D supports	¾"	4"	5½"	BP	2
PUSHBLOCK					
E handle	1¹⁄₁₆"	3¼"	4½"	B	1
F base	¾"	5½"	7"	B	1
G fence	¾"	1"	8"	B	1
RIGHT-ANGLE SUPPORT					
H mounting plate	¼"	1¾"	5¼"	BP	1
I support	¾"	5¼"	7½"	BP	1
FEATHER BOARDS					
J long one	¾"	2⅜"	18"	B	1
K short one	¾"	2⅜"	8¾"	B	1
L support	¾"	¾"	9½"	B	1

Material Key: BP—birch plywood, B—birch

Supplies: #8X¾" flathead wood screws, #8X1¼" flathead wood screws, #8X1½" flathead wood screws, 3—¼X¾" roundhead machine screws with 3—¼" flat washers and 3—¼" T-nuts, ½" dowel stock, ¼" acrylic for dust cover and guard, acrylic solvent cement, clear finish.

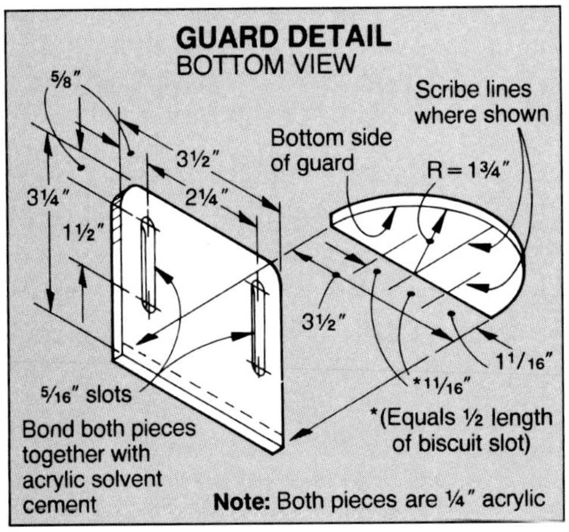

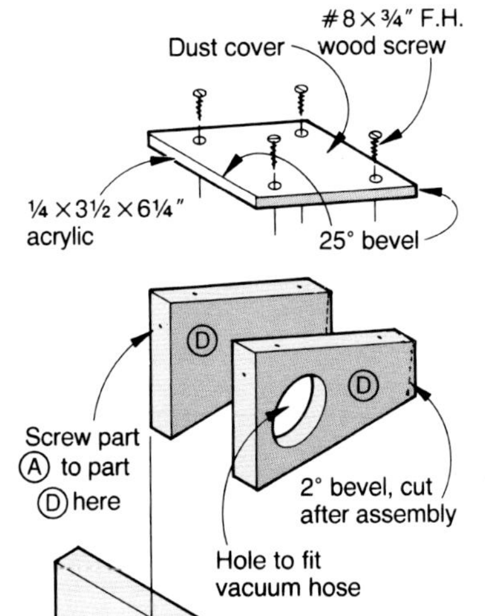

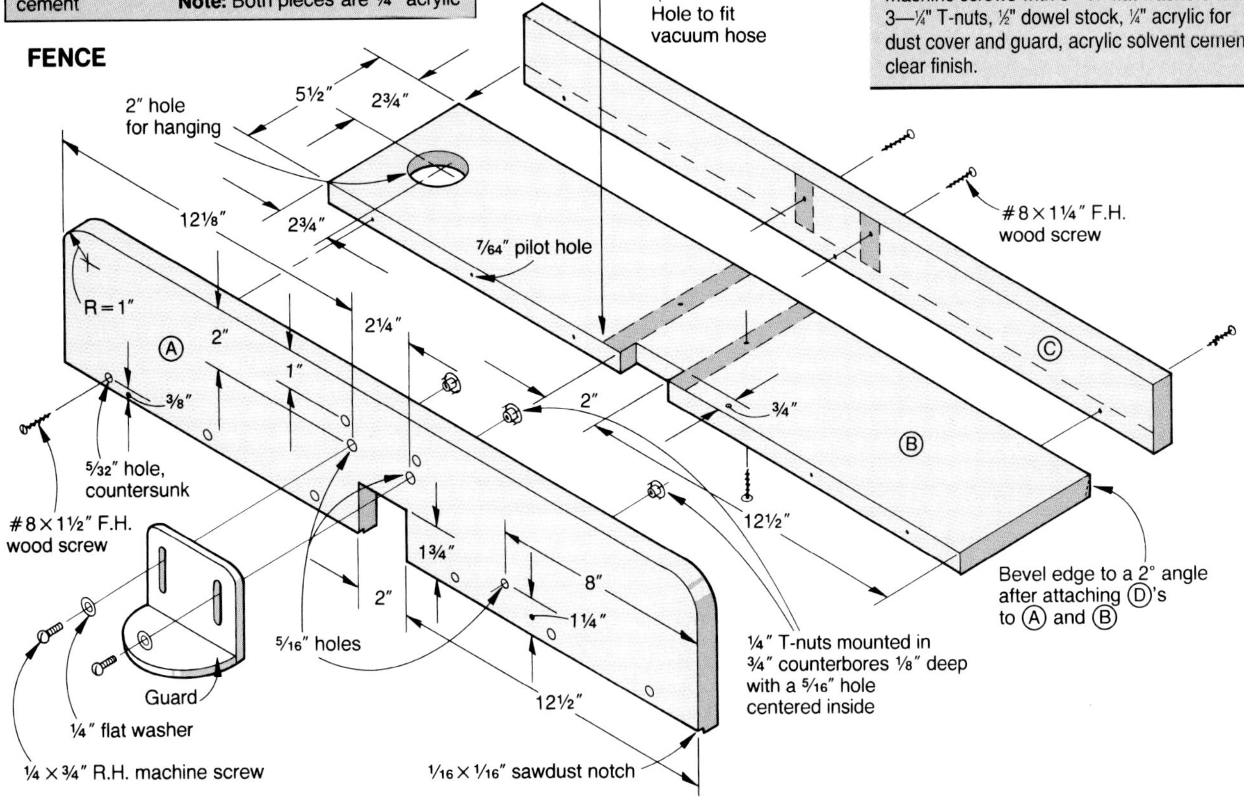

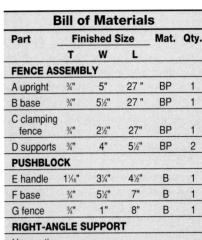

THE ULTIMATE ROUTER FENCE SYSTEM

continued

the Parts View drawing for the full-sized pattern of part H.

2. Drill a pair of 5⁄16" holes in the mounting plates, and then cut the waste between the holes to form the slot where shown in the Right-Angle Support drawing.

3. Drill the mounting holes, and glue and screw the two pieces together where shown *above right*.

4. Bore a ¾" hole in the support for hanging.

Add the guard and the finish

1. Using the Guard detail accompanying the Fence drawing on *page 73* for reference, cut the two guard pieces to shape from ¼" acrylic.

2. Scribe the slot locations where shown on the detail, and then drill a 5⁄16" hole at each end of each slot. (Since acrylic is hard to mark, we applied masking tape onto the acrylic, and marked the slot lines on the tape.) Scrollsaw the material between the holes to form the slots.

3. On the *bottom* face of the rounded piece of acrylic, scribe a centerline and two cutter end

PUSH BLOCK

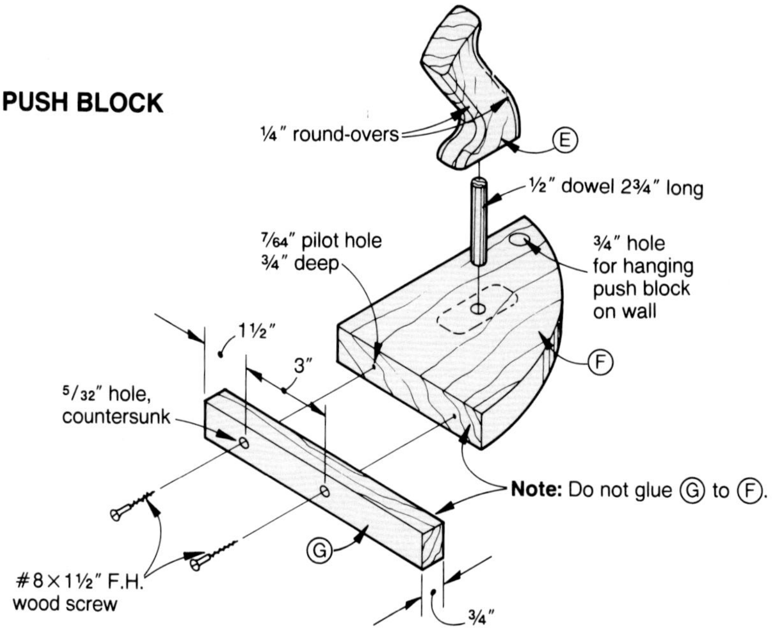
¼" round-overs
E
½" dowel 2¾" long
7⁄64" pilot hole
¾" deep
¾" hole
for hanging
push block
on wall
1½"
3"
F
5⁄32" hole,
countersunk
Note: Do not glue G to F.
G
#8 × 1½" F.H.
wood screw
¾"

RIGHT-ANGLE SUPPORT

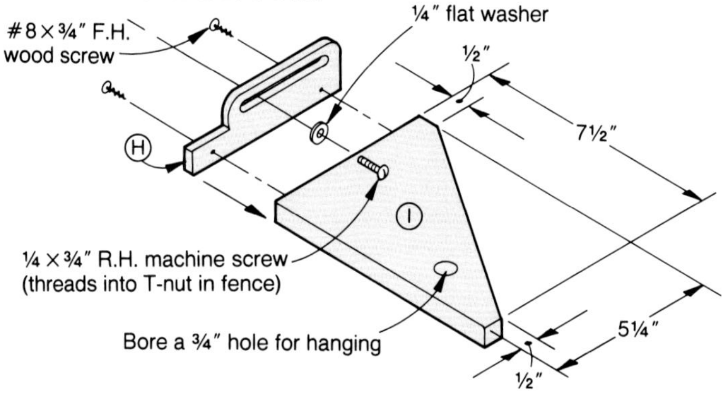
#8 × ¾" F.H.
wood screw
¼" flat washer
½"
7½"
H
I
¼ × ¾" R.H. machine screw
(threads into T-nut in fence)
Bore a ¾" hole for hanging
5¼"
½"

Router-Fence System Safety Guard

Our fence works great for routing a smooth, straight edge. For edges that curve gently, use the ends of the side pieces (A) as guide pins for support when starting and stopping the cut. For an edge with more exaggerated curves, like that shown *right*, move the guard back slightly and work directly off the piloted bit.

Beyond its basic uses, our guard excels as an effective chip-collection hood. And, more important, it lets you safely see your work during the routing operation without worrying about particles flying into your eyes.

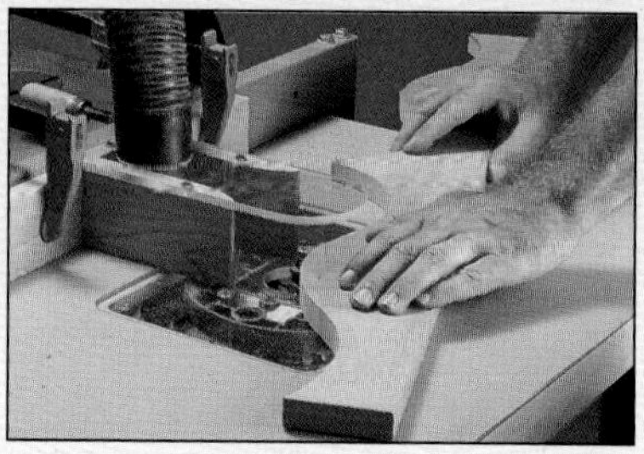

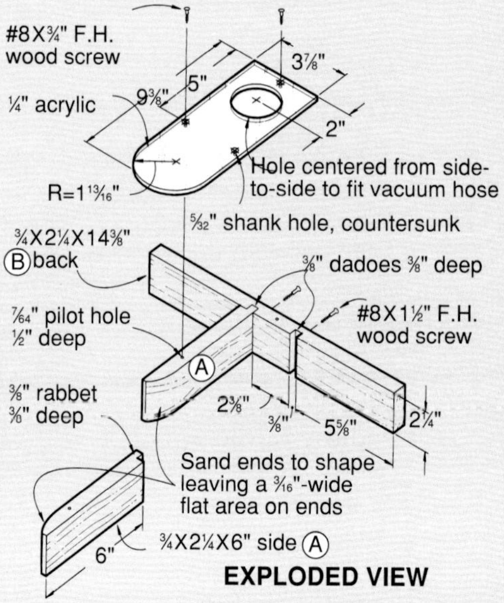
#8X¾" F.H.
wood screw
3⅞"
¼" acrylic
9⅜"
5"
2"
Hole centered from side-to-side to fit vacuum hose
R=1 13⁄16"
5⁄32" shank hole, countersunk
¾X2¼X14⅜"
B back
⅜" dadoes ⅜" deep
7⁄64" pilot hole
½" deep
#8X1½" F.H.
wood screw
A
⅜" rabbet
⅜" deep
2⅜"
⅜"
5⅝"
2¼"
Sand ends to shape
leaving a 3⁄16"-wide
flat area on ends
6"
¾X2¼X6" side A
EXPLODED VIEW

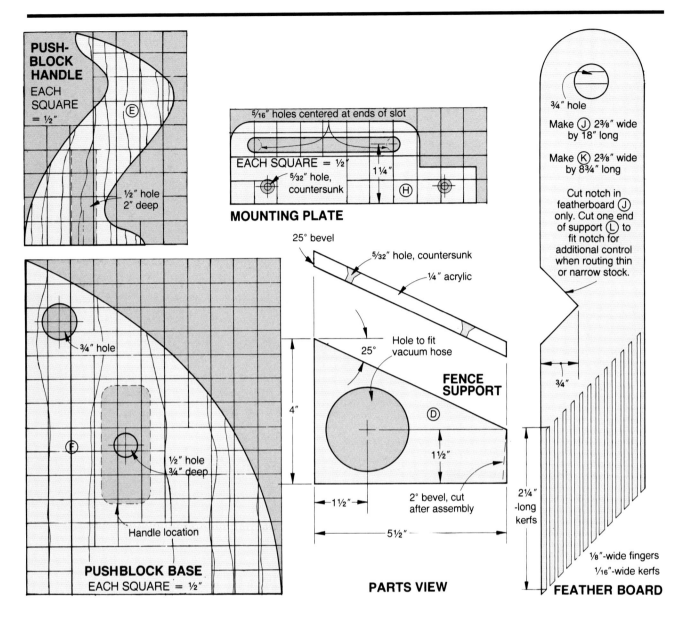

PUSH-BLOCK HANDLE
EACH SQUARE = ½"

E

½" hole
2" deep

5/16" holes centered at ends of slot

EACH SQUARE = ½"

5/32" hole, countersunk

1¼"

H

MOUNTING PLATE

25° bevel

5/32" hole, countersunk

¼" acrylic

¾" hole

½" hole
¾" deep

F

Handle location

PUSHBLOCK BASE
EACH SQUARE = ½"

Hole to fit
vacuum hose

25°

**FENCE
SUPPORT**

D

4"

1½"

1½"

5½"

2° bevel, cut
after assembly

PARTS VIEW

¾" hole

Make (J) 2⅜" wide
by 18" long

Make (K) 2⅜" wide
by 8¾" long

Cut notch in
featherboard (J)
only. Cut one end
of support (L) to
fit notch for
additional control
when routing thin
or narrow stock.

¾"

2¼"
-long
kerfs

⅛"-wide fingers
1/16"-wide kerfs

FEATHER BOARD

alignment lines on the acrylic. As shown in the drawing *right,* we used the *back* edge of an X-ACTO knife. We found it difficult to scribe a straight line using the cutting edge of the knife. The distance between the alignment marks should be equal to the length of the biscuit slot cut with the biscuit cutter.

4. To make the scribed lines stand out and easier to see, highlight them with a marking pen.

5. Hold the pieces squarely together, and use acrylic solvent cement to bond the two pieces of acrylic to finish forming the guard.

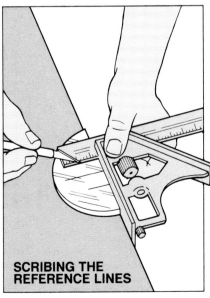

**SCRIBING THE
REFERENCE LINES**

Time for the feather boards and finish

1. Using the Feather Board drawing for reference, cut one long and two short feather boards (J, K) and a feather-board support (L) to size and shape.

2. Mark the locations and use your bandsaw to cut 1/16" kerfs 2¼" long where shown on the Feather Board drawing.

3. Mark the centerpoints, and bore a ¾" hole in the radiused end of each feather board. Use the holes later when hanging the feather boards between use.

4. Add a clear finish to all the wood parts. Later, attach the guard to the upright (A) and the dust cover to the supports (D).

DRILL PRESS COLLECTOR DUST

Wood chips and sawdust don't stay around long when you hook up this clamp-down collector to your shop vacuum or dust-collection system. You'll breathe a lot easier and cut down cleanup time, too.

Use the Exploded View and Parts View drawings to construct the collector from ¼" plywood and ¾" stock. Cut or sand 10° bevels across the top and sides of the ¾"-thick back where shown *below*. To reduce sawdust buildup at table level, sand a bevel across the front edge of the bottom piece.

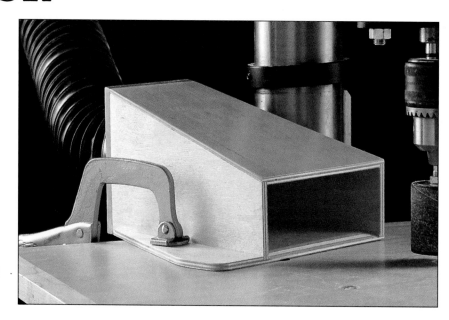

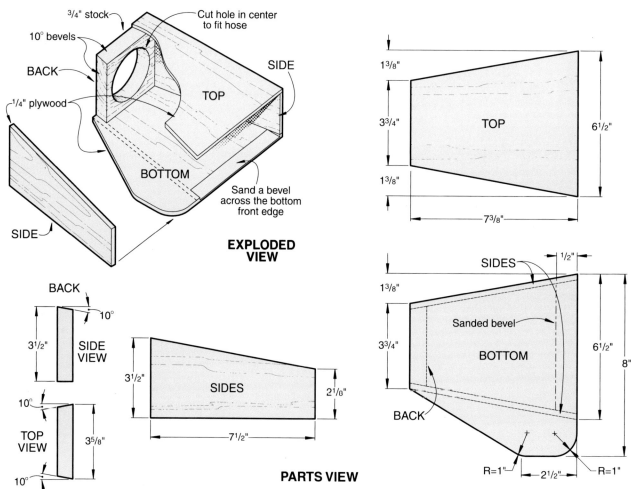

EXPLODED VIEW

PARTS VIEW

SWING-ARM SUPPORT

Keep the motor end of your rotary tool up and out of the way and the flexible-shaft and business end close at hand with this convenient swing-arm support. We centered ours over one of our Idea Shop™ workbenches where we plan to do a lot of carving.

After using the tool, just loop the end of the flexible shaft through one of the holes in the swing-arm support and then swing the arm to one side until you need it again.

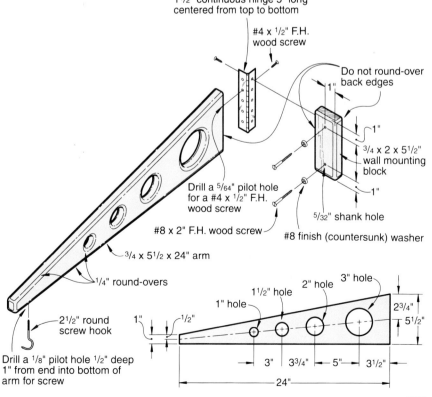

1¹/₂" continuous hinge 5" long centered from top to bottom

#4 x ¹/₂" F.H. wood screw

Do not round-over back edges

1"

1"

³/₄ x 2 x 5¹/₂" wall mounting block

1"

Drill a ⁵/₆₄" pilot hole for a #4 x ¹/₂" F.H. wood screw

#8 x 2" F.H. wood screw

⁵/₃₂" shank hole

#8 finish (countersunk) washer

³/₄ x 5¹/₂ x 24" arm

¹/₄" round-overs

2¹/₂" round screw hook

Drill a ¹/₈" pilot hole ¹/₂" deep 1" from end into bottom of arm for screw

1" hole   1¹/₂" hole   2" hole   3" hole

1"   ¹/₂"   2³/₄"   5¹/₂"

3"   3³/₄"   5"   3¹/₂"

24"

SAFETY IS JOB ONE

Good woodworking begins with good habits, and here we offer simple, practical guidelines to keep you healthy and safe while you work in your shop.

FOUR CORNERSTONES OF SHOP SAFETY

Despite the best intentions, more than 300,000 persons rush to hospital emergency rooms each year, victims of serious home workshop accidents. On top of that, says the National Safety Council, two to three times that number go unreported. We think these sobering statistics are reason enough to offer you a short shop safety review. Teachers, experienced woodworkers—even your dad—no doubt passed along safety guidelines on numerous occasions. Our five safety experts spell them out again, because they're worth repeating, again and again.

Rule 1: Keep a shipshape shop

"Good workshop lighting is essential. Light fixtures should provide clear vision with a minimum of shadows in work areas and over machines," says Phil Schmidt, section head, National Safety Council.

Besides adequate light, Schmidt advises you to set up your shop to allow ample space for your stationary tools. "There should be no danger of bumping into one machine while using another," he says.

Minimize tripping, slipping, or falling by stowing idle tools and sweeping up around your machines every 30 minutes or so. To avoid cuts and splinters, clear saw tabletops of sawdust and scraps with a brush or shop vacuum, rather than your bare hands, suggests the NSC staff. And, store materials and parts out of the way.

Always turn off and unplug machines while adjusting them and changing blades or bits. But never unplug a power tool by giving the cord a jerk and never drag a tool around by its cord. This eventually wears on the connection.

Make sure everything is electrically safe, too, the NSC says. All power tools should have three-pronged plugs, except double-insulated tools. And install ground-fault circuit interrupters (they may be required by your local electrical code). Finally, check *continued*

FOUR CORNERSTONES OF SHOP SAFETY
continued

for underpowered circuits over-loaded by numerous power tools.

Rule 2: Dress for woodworking success

"Watch those precious eyes—you have two for a lifetime!" says Bob Hempy, product planning manager, Delta. "The sharp, spinning steel of a table saw, the grit of a sander, the wood bits from a lathe, dictate that you wear safety glasses or goggles that provide side protection with shields," emphasizes Hempy. "Eye protection is always a must, even with most hand tools. And, you need a face mask for dust protection."

Heber Anderson, Black & Decker's product training manager, says, "People have actually died by getting a tie caught and pulled into a lathe. So, dress appropriately. Avoid wearing loose clothing, long sleeves, jewelry, and gloves while working with power tools, particularly lathes and routers."

Adds the NSC's Schmidt, "Keep long hair out of the way with a close-fitting cap or net. Shoes with rubber soles provide better support and protection from slipping, as well as from sharp objects on the floor. If there's a danger of heavy objects falling on your feet in your shop, wear industrial-type shoes with steel safety toes."

Protect your hearing with disposable earplugs, reusable earplugs, or cushioned muffs when you use power saws, jointers, or routers. Some routers, for instance, can exceed the 85-decibel threshold for hearing loss established by OSHA, the government's industrial safety watchdog. While you would have to endure that high pitch for several hours to sustain injury, with all the other noise you subject your ears to, why take chances?

Rule 3: Respect your tools

According to Heber Anderson, "If you get into a 40-tooth saw blade turning at 5,800 rpm, more than 1,288 teeth will pass through

your hand before you can move it." Vivid facts instill caution, states Anderson. "If everyone thought of that saw blade in terms of what all those teeth can do, they'd pay a tablesaw more respect," he says.

Overconfidence contributes to accidents, according to Anderson. "We see people who have handled tools all their lives become almost as dangerous as a novice," he says with great concern.

Delta's Hempy couldn't agree more. "Lack of respect for the machine, repetitive work, and working with the blade guard removed often result in a finger or hand in the blade."

Another Delta safety professional, Mat Ros, product safety manager, suggests ways to avoid potentially nasty tablesaw accidents:
• Leave the blade guard on when sawing.
• Use protective jigs, feather boards, and push sticks.
• Don't rip boards without clamping the rip fence.
• Avoid blade binding or kicking by only making crosscuts with the help of the miter gauge.

• Never reach around or over the blade.

Making tools do a job they weren't designed to do causes injuries, too. "For example," says Jim Elmore, Stanley Tool Division's manager of product safety, "people commonly use a screwdriver for a pry bar, and it can break."

Beware of dull cutting tools, too. A dull saw blade overheats, sticks, and kicks more than a sharp one.

Rule 4: Give woodworking your attention

"The poor guy who's just had a spat with a family member and goes down into the basement to work in his shop is apt to do something the wrong way," says Jim Elmore.

"When you're emotionally upset, let the tools lie. If you're overtired or feeling ill, don't try to work. These are common sense things that people overlook sometimes for the sake of getting the project done," notes Elmore.

"Inattentiveness and distractions can lead to disaster," agrees the NSC's Schmidt. "Concentrate on the

task at hand and don't rush through it, even when you feel hurried."

To break up the monotony of making repetitive cuts, stop and do something else for awhile. Also, insist that no visitors disrupt you. In particular, keep small children out of your shop at all times, especially while you're busy working.

The NSC insists that you stay out of the shop when you're under the influence of alcohol or any medication that affects your alertness or ability to function normally. And, smoking while using tools isn't recommended either. Distractions, such as smoke in your eyes or dropping a cigarette at a critical time, could result in injury.

HOW SAFE ARE YOUR WOODWORKING HABITS?

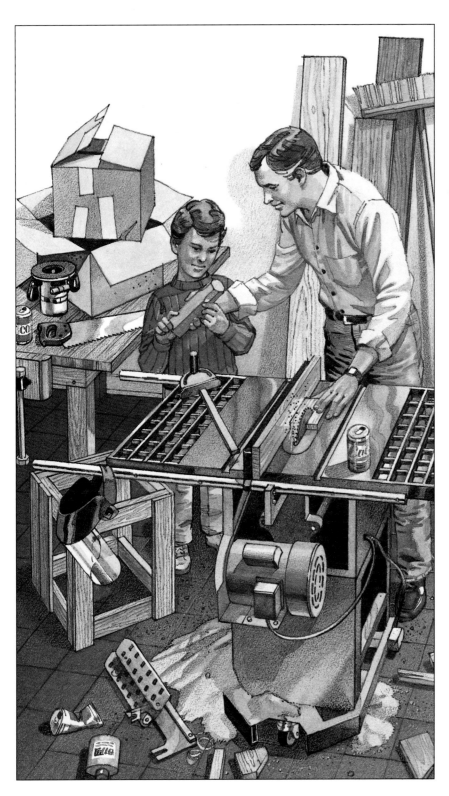

All of us here at *WOOD*® want you to enjoy your wood-working hobby for years to come. We invite you to use the 14 photographs shown on the following pages to test your safety savvy. Look over each situation carefully, and jot down anything that doesn't look quite right. Then, compare your notes with the answers that appear *below* and on *page 85*.

What's your safety IQ?

Chalk up one point for each mistake that you caught and we described. Total your score and see the ratings on *page 85*.

Bonus points: If you noticed that our man's clothing was dangerously loose in several pictures, give yourself an extra point. And, if you noted his jewelry and thought he'd be better off without it, score another point.

1. Always unplug your router before changing bits. And, clean clutter out of the way. If this router were to rock against the adjustable clamp, the switch could click ON.

2. Nice goggles, but it's not the top of your head we're most concerned about here. Always put them over your eyes. Also, clamp that board securely, and chuck the entire router shank into the collet.

3. No matter how steady your hands are, they're not as steady as a tool rest. Lower that shield in place, too. And while you're at it, pop a bulb
continued

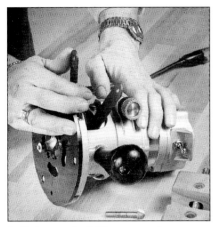

1. Got a router? If so, you change router bits now and then. Do you see anything wrong with the way it's being done here?

2. With the bit securely locked in the collet, you're ready to rout.

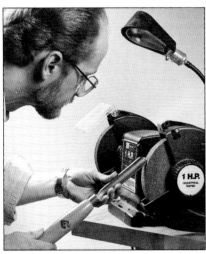

3. Aah, you say, nothing could be simpler than touching up the edge of a cutting tool on a grinder. We beg to differ.

4. One last finishing touch with the gouge and your decorative carving will be done. But try to finish without hurting yourself.

6. The advantage of plywood is that it comes in big sheets. That's also the disadvantage. Find a better way to make rough cuts.

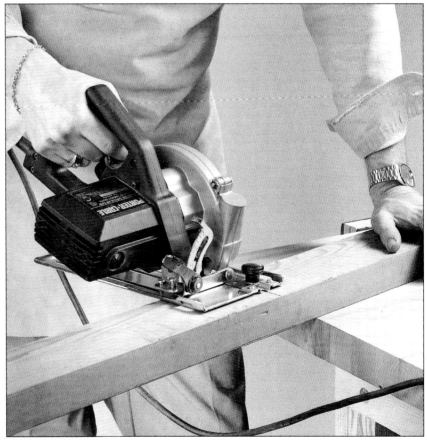

5. Another common and simple procedure—cutting off a board. Still, there's a right way and a wrong way, and this isn't the right way.

HOW SAFE ARE YOUR WOODWORKING HABITS?
continued

7. It's so easy to turn on the belt sander and quickly remove stock. But what risks do you run?

8. You operate the tablesaw so much that you assume you're using it safely, right?

9. Back to the tablesaw again. Now, let's put that popular material, plywood, through the tablesaw, and see how two "populars" create problems for some woodworkers.

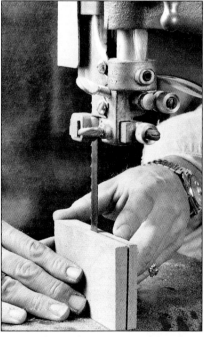

10. Bandsaws have a nasty bite if you aren't careful.

11. It is so tempting to make quick work of boring some dowel holes with the drill press. But you know where temptation leads.

12. A radial-arm saw is an efficient machine for cross-cutting, ripping, and—if you handle it like this—for injury, too.

13. Here, you see a thickness planer with the power ON and our woodworker with his thinking circuits OFF. Even though you may not have this power tool in your shop, what would you do differently to avoid a trip to the emergency room?

14. Let's close with a classic. This woodworker is running a 9" long piece of stock through the jointer. What safety rules is he violating?

into that fixture. Oops! Don't forget to wear those goggles!

4. Experienced carvers know the importance of clamping down the workpiece. First, doing so prevents the work from moving around. And second, clamps allow you to keep your free hand away from the tool.

5. This situation cries out for clamps. And, get the power cord away from the cutting path of the blade.

6. Lots of errors here: Failure to support and clamp the end of the panel, overreaching, and neglecting to keep the power cord out of the saw kerf. By the way, pardon our careless woodworker if he thinks it's kind of foggy in his shop—he hasn't cleaned his face shield in weeks.

7. Don't let the smooth look of a sanding belt fool you. Keep your fingers well away. This is no place for a tie, jewelry, or a loose coat.

8. If you're looking for a place to store tools, scraps, and project pieces, the tablesaw isn't it. Other

mistakes: Feeding the stock with the fingers instead of a push stick, and neglecting to use a clamped-down feather board to hold stock.

9. Without a helper or solid support under the far end of the plywood, this woodworker may lose control of the workpiece. First, rough-cut sheets with a portable circular saw rather than a tablesaw. Clear the area of all obstructions including power cords, wood scraps, and items that may prevent the completion of the cut.

10. At this moment, our woodworker has two intact thumbs. If he continues, that could change. Use a block to push this piece. Also, lower the blade guard for safety and to keep the blade from wandering off the mark.

11. Keep your chuck key nearby— but not in the chuck. And next time, clamp the stock securely.

12. The sight of a hand close to a saw blade should give you a chill. Always use a push stick.

And, don't forget to lower the anti-kickback arm and tilt the hood.

13. Our man is risking his eyes and facial injury by looking inside while the planer is running, and he's risking his hand by reaching into the machine to push the stock through. Stop the machine and unplug it before getting anywhere near the cutterheads. And, never raise or lower the table during the cut.

14. Never, never, never feed any board shorter than 12" long through a jointer. To prevent your hand from contacting the cutters, use a pushblock or pushstick, and secure loose clothing.

Now, score yourself

28—36: Safety Ace. You're alert and well-informed. Don't ease up.

20—27: Stitch in Time. A careless act could send you to the emergency room. Please study those items that you missed.

19 or less: An Accident Waiting to Happen. Your next shop project should be a safety session.

SPOTLIGHT ON TABLESAW SAFETY

Safety statisticians associate the tablesaw with more home-workshop accidents than any other woodworking power tool. But common sense and proven practices, such as those found here, pay big safety dividends.

According to the U.S. Consumer Product Safety Commission's 1991 compilation from their National Electronic Injury Surveillance System (NEISS), injuries treated at emergency rooms said to be associated with table- or benchtop-model saws were estimated at 30,091. Five percent of these patients required hospitalization. That's at least 15 times the number of accidents related to radial-arm saws or routers, making the tablesaw the number one threat among woodworking power tools.

That unfortunate role may be due to other factors, such as the number of tablesaws owned and the amount they're used. But neither of these probable reasons change the statistics.

"I see about 20 people a year who are home woodworkers, and whether or not it was the tablesaw they were using, they all say, 'It happened so fast,'" comments Delwin E. Quenzer, M.D., a leading orthopedic surgeon in Des Moines, Iowa. "And all of them feel remorse because they know the accident was avoidable." See the box, *right,* for his recommendations for prevention.

You can also avert becoming another injury statistic by reading, then practicing, the following rules and techniques of tablesaw use developed by expert woodworkers for the National Safety Council. And don't just be aware of them, make safety a habit.

Sage advice on saw safety

Of course, you'll want to dress appropriately—and safely—when working in the shop, as suggested in the box, *opposite, top.* Then, always heed these general rules:

• Once the saw is in motion, never reach over or around it.

• Clear the area around the tablesaw from scrap, including dust.

• Create safe footing by standing on a nonskid mat.

• Choose the right saw blade for the job. Don't use a crosscut blade for ripping or vice versa.

And, to prevent sudden surprises, remember to:

• Unplug power tools when changing or adjusting blades.

• Lower the tablesaw blade below table height when not in use.

• Always clear off the table with a brush or whisk broom, not with the palm of your hand.

But, when it comes to specific operations, you'll need to be even more careful. Take ripping, for instance, the most common tablesaw chore.

Ripping: Dangerous at all times

The National Safety Council advises that it's during ripping that most accidents occur. Here's how to protect yourself:

• Allow 3' of clear area at the working end of the saw (where you stand), plus the length of the stock you're ripping.

• Before sawing, set the blade teeth to proper height. Blades with a set, or flat ground blades, should extend no more than one tooth-height above the wood. Carbide-tipped blade teeth should extend no more than half of a tooth-height. Raise hollow-ground or planer blades as far as possible above the work to avoid binding.

• Keep your hands and body out of line with the cut. Try this to keep your pushing hand out of the blade: Hook the small and ring fingers of the pushing hand over the fence (if without obstruction) to slide with the wood.

• Saw with your weight equally balanced on both feet, gripping the stock firmly but not crowding it

The Doctor's Orders

Dr. Quenzer, whose patients come from industry and the home, cites all the "risk factors" that contribute to most power-tool accidents, especially tablesaws:

• Working tired, upset, angry, depressed, or when taking alcohol or prescription drugs.

• Carelessness, such as loss of attention during repetitive cuts.

• Removing or not using safety equipment, including blade guards and pushsticks.

• Not maintaining shop equipment, and using dull, burnt, or gummy blades that cause binding and kickback.

• Working with small children around. Or worse, allowing them in the shop in the absence of adult supervision.

The doctor also believes that accidents happen when people push their machines. "There are limits to what you can expect a piece of equipment to do," he says. He points out, for example, that many tablesaw injuries result from trying to rip too small a piece of wood.

and the blade. If the work should give, you don't want to be pulled into the blade.

• Never rip without the fence nor crosscut without the miter gauge.

• When ripping short or narrow stock, rely on a pushstick rather than your hands. If possible, rip narrow strips with the wider stock against the rip fence (or follow the suggestion illustrated *below*). Thin pieces can catch between the fence and the blade and fly back.

• Rip long stock only with adequate support beyond the blade, such as an off-feed table or roller.

Special cuts mean caution, too:

• Because stock has a tendency to creep toward the blade during a miter cut, clamp the workpiece in place on the miter gauge.

• Crosscut small pieces only with the workpiece safely supported by an auxiliary miter-gauge fence.

• Blind-cutting, as in groove-ripping or dadoing, is dangerous. Always clamp stops to auxiliary fences to regulate the beginning and end of a cut.

• Never make a cut that you have the slightest doubt about.

Dress for success

Fashion doesn't dictate your woodworking attire, safety does. The wrong type of clothes can cause accidents. Be comfortable, but heed the following advice:

• Protect your eyes with goggles or safety glasses equipped with side shields.

• Wear hearing protection such as muffs or plugs.

• Roll long sleeves above the elbow or wear a short-sleeved shirt.

• Remove all jewelry, such as wristwatches, bracelets, or cumbersome rings.

• Prevent slipping by wearing shoes with rubber soles.

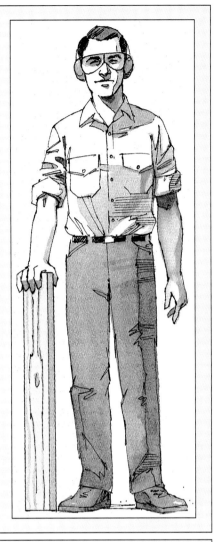

How to rip thin pieces safely

Jim Boelling, *WOOD*® magazine's project builder, regularly rips stock into thin pieces as shown. "The large pushblock enables you to hold the stock solidly against the table as it goes through and exits the blade. It's great for repetitive cuts."

According to Jim, the secret to success is to first dimension the stock to desired thickness, then rip it to width. "Be sure you cut the notch in the bottom of the solid pushblock to exactly match your stock's thickness," he adds. "That means making a new pushblock for each thickness of wood you want to rip, but it's worth it. And even without the blade guard, it's a safe operation."

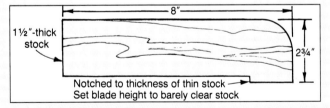

8"

1½"-thick stock

2¾"

Notched to thickness of thin stock →
Set blade height to barely clear stock

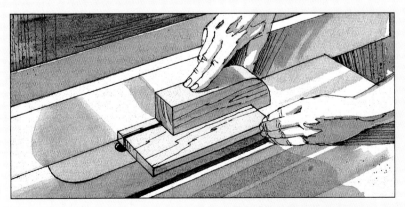

KEEP SAFETY IN SIGHT

Don't have illusions about protecting your eyes. According to the National Society to Prevent Blindness, hospital emergency rooms annually treat at least 35,000 people for eye injuries received in the home workshop! Jim Boelling, *above,* our Project Builder at *WOOD* ® Magazine, once nearly counted himself among the statistics. "I was working for the local school district in their furniture factory," Jim recalls. "The union required us to wear both eye and ear protection. So, I was wearing my safety glasses one afternoon when I started up the

big, straight-line saw to rip 2×2" table legs from rough, 8/4 oak. As I turned to feed more board into the blade, it happened. WHAM! My glasses exploded off my face and dropped. I heard tinkles like a handful of buck-shot on a tin roof as carbide flew everywhere. A chunk of barbed wire buried in the wood had fractured 14 of the 28 carbide teeth on that saw!" he exclaims. "One tiny piece of carbide had hit the edge of the lens, chipping it. My optometrist said the carbide would have penetrated my eye socket and probably killed me if I hadn't worn my safety glasses. To this day, I can't help viewing thick boards with suspicion—through safety glasses!"

Whatever excuse you might have for not wearing eye protection in the shop, it won't hold up. Today's standard lineup of safety glasses presents dozens of style and comfort options to fit all budgets. However, when it comes to a standard of protection, there's only one.

"Real" safety glasses have a pedigree

"Real" safety glasses must meet ANSI Z87.1-1979 ("Z87" for short), the performance standard for protective eyewear set by the American National Standards Institute (ANSI). ANSI, a voluntary organization, coordinates the development of standards used in business, industry, government, and educational institutions. It wrote the Z87 standard for the workplace. But, your home workshop differs only in size, not in the number of possible hazards you risk.

Most safety glasses or goggles manufactured after 1979 that meet Z87 will have that fact right on them. Look at the lenses (usually in the top center or outside edges at top and bottom). As shown in the top photo, *opposite,* each lens

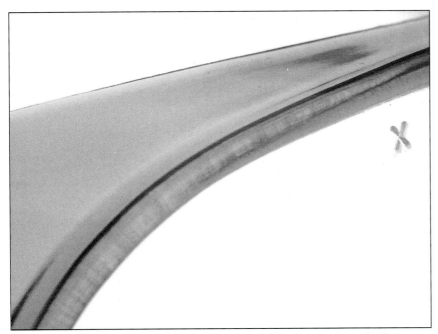

Genuine safety glasses carry the manufacturer's monogram on the lenses.

Frames that meet the Z87 standard usually carry this marking.

displays the manufacturer's monogram or trademark—such as TO for Titmus®, AO for American Optical, X for UVEX, VC for Pearle Vision Center. Inspect the frame on the front and temple or ear pieces and you'll see a Z87, *below left.* Older glasses may only carry the lens marking.

Although these markings generally hold true in indicating compliance with Z87, a few very contemporary, wraparound styles, though completely safe, carry no marking at all. Kathy Peterson, a spokesperson for American Optical, maker of the "Saf Scanner," a one-piece molded model of safety eyewear, explains: "ANSI sets the minimum performance standard for designs of glasses with a frame and two lenses. Our Saf Scanners are of one-piece construction. They meet or exceed ANSI Z87. But, because of the design, we cannot imprint the designation on them."

Lenses and frames: Partners in safety

Both the frame and the lenses of safety glasses work together for the utmost protection. If only one partner meets the standard, the pair won't protect you.

For instance, the lens might not shatter under an impact. The impact, though, could drive the lens *out of a regular frame and into your eye!* Lenses in plastic safety frames must be mounted from the front with a strong retention lip to prevent them from projecting back into the eye. Metal frames use an equally effective lens insertion.

Warning: Don't confuse "impact-resistant" lenses with industrial-quality safety glasses. Regular prescription (Rx) glasses are, by law, required to be impact-resistant. However, safety glasses must withstand nearly four times the impact (in foot-pounds of pressure) of regular prescription glasses.

continued

KEEP SAFETY IN SIGHT
continued

Frames for regular glasses have no strength or impact requirements to protect you. But safety frames, like safety lenses, must tolerate pressure and impact from the front and sides. Metal frames, for example, must show no cracks or solder breaks after being bent in half until the lenses touch, and then straightened.

Your options in safety eyewear

Top-notch eye protection should be your only consideration when it comes to selecting eyewear.

Your eyesight, however, partially determines your style options. For instance, if you don't require corrective lenses, you can choose (1) goggles, (2) prefabricated safety eyewear *(prefabs)* with noncorrective clear *(plano)* safety lenses already in place, or (3) safety frames in which plano safety lenses are inserted.

If you need corrective lenses, you can (1) wear goggles or prefabs designed to be worn over your regular glasses, or (2) order prescription safety glasses made.

Contact lens wearers can (1) wear their contacts protected by goggles, prefabs, or safety glasses with plano lenses, or (2) remove contacts and wear prescription safety glasses instead. Note: Contact lenses—either hard or soft—*do not protect* your eyes. Never wear them in shop situations without adequate safety eyewear.

The cost of quality protection

Surprisingly, protection at the Z87 level starts at $1.89, and may go as high as $100. Generally, at the lower end of the scale you're trading off some optical clarity in the lenses and custom fit. On the high end, you'll get glasses you can wear in the shop and out to dinner, too.

Prefabricated plano safety eyewear, either as glasses or in a wrap-around style, comes ready to wear with plano lenses in place for $4 to $25. Prefabs offer many choices in style: (1) regular spectacle look-alikes with side shields that may or may not be removable, (2) ones that wrap around your face, giving you wider peripheral vision, and (3) glasses in which the shields are an integral part of a plastic frame.

You can wear some prefabs over prescription glasses. Others have adjustable temples or come in more than one size. When you purchase prefabs from an eyewear specialist, the specialist usually can make some adjustments for a better fit.

In general, you'll pay more for "prefabs" that have frames and lenses of the same quality as regular glasses. The quality of the optics usually ascends with the price, although some pairs for $5 still have good optics.

Prescription safety glasses give you a custom fit, usually the clearest look at your work, and, if you choose, a pair of glasses you could wear all the time (with side shields removed). Prices for most safety frames fitted with single-vision prescription safety lenses range from $30 for a not-so-stylish pair to $60 for plastic-framed glasses (bifocals and trifocals cost more) that look as handsome as any fashion pair. Some plastic-framed and metal-framed pairs soar to the $100 level.

A few safety glasses have permanently attached side shields; some have no shields. Most safety glasses, though, can be fitted with side shields. Side shields provide you with 20 to 25 percent more protection than safety glasses alone, according to Dr. Joseph F. Novak, a University of Pennsylvania clinical professor of ophthalmology and eye-safety consultant to U.S. Steel. And, shields add only $1 to $5 to the price. The bottom line: Buy shields and wear them.

Goggle-eyed over safety

Fitting closely to your face, goggles give you the best impact protection from every angle. They're the safe choice when you work with chemicals, such as strippers. Many goggles with an adjustable elastic band fit easily over regular glasses. Neoprene head straps may be used with chemical goggles.

And yes, some goggles even prove comfortable worn over prescription glasses. But at only $2 to about $10, goggles won't be the highest quality optical product. What you see may be a little fuzzy. "Seeing with a slight distortion through goggles won't harm your eyes. Instead, it will save them," reminds Dr. Novak. We found, by the way, that goggle optical quality does vary greatly between brands and price ranges.

Safety lenses—a tough match for steel wool

Both plastic and glass lenses can meet the Z87 standard. However, plastic—specifically *polycarbonate* plastic—receives the highest recommendation from a safety standpoint from a majority of manufacturers. Polycarbonate tops glass and CR-39®, another high-quality plastic, for impact resistance.

You'll find that plastic lenses have greater impact resistance than glass. They're also lighter. And although plastic lenses do pit and scratch easier than their glass equivalent, this won't reduce their impact resistance as with glass.

You should always ask for "scratch-resistant" lenses. Scratch resistance, like safety lenses, has come a long way. For example, in Titmus® test comparisons, their scratch-resistant lenses are eight times more resistant to scratching from a pencil than uncoated lenses. At Pearle Laboratories, the scratch-resistant lenses test 15 times more resistant than untreated ones when rubbed with 0000 steel wool!

How to deal with multiple distances

If you want to see to saw safely, you may need bi- or trifocals. If your regular glasses, for instance, magnify so you can see clearly close up, but your vision gets fuzzy when you work at the tablesaw, you can get one pair of safety glasses made to cover both distances. Consult an ophthalmologist or optometrist about your specific distance problem. He or she can write a prescription that will correct for two or three distances.

Another option: If you almost exclusively do one type of woodworking at a single distance—such as lathe turning—you can get single-vision safety glasses or bifocals corrected to a specific distance(s).

Your prescription for correction won't specify safety glasses. That's up to you to request. Simply order frames and lenses that meet ΛNSI Z87. When your glasses arrive, inspect them for the manufacturer's monogram on the lenses and the Z87 imprinted on the frames.

Note: *You won't always find safety glasses on display because they rarely account for a large percentage of sales. Ask for them.*

Stop your glasses from attracting sawdust

Static electricity attracts sawdust to lenses, especially plastic ones. Dennis Tumminello, a woodworker

who heads Pearle Laboratories in Dallas, has the solution: "Start with scratch-resistant lenses for some antistatic protection. Then clean them with ArmorAll®, a product available at hardware stores."

Where to buy safety glasses

• *Hardware stores and home centers* sell goggles and prefab safety eyewear. However, all of their products may not meet the Z87 standard, so read labels and warnings carefully.

• *Opticians and optical centers,* such as Pearle Vision Centers, Sterling Optical, and others, fill prescriptions, make prescription safety glasses, sell safety glasses with plano lenses, and sell prefab safety glasses. Some, with affiliated optometrists, also write prescriptions.

• *Optometrists* usually provide the services of opticians and optical centers, plus they test your eyes. *Ophthalmologists* are doctors of medicine who also prescribe corrective lenses. Some will dispense glasses; others only provide the prescription you fill elsewhere.

• *Safety specialty stores* carry goggles and prefabs and from bulk often will break out a single pair for you. Find them in the Yellow Pages under "Safety Equipment."

THE WOODWORKER'S SURVIVAL GUIDE TO BUYING RESPIRATORS

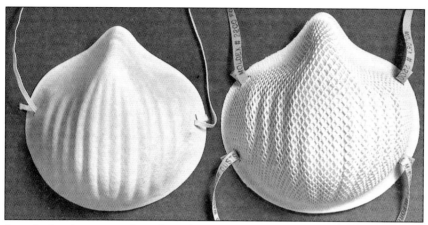

A typical nuisance mask such as the one *at left* has one strap and a thinner filter material than its NIOSH/MSHA-approved counterpart *at right*.

L ike many of you, I make every attempt to collect sawdust at its source. And, when I'm finishing or refinishing a project, I always ventilate a room. But no matter how hard I try, some sawdust and vapors always wind up in the air. Since I don't like to gamble with my health, I decided to get the lowdown on respirators. Now, I know what products will protect my lungs, and I'm breathing a whole lot easier.

—*Bill Krier*
Products/Techniques Editor

When do you need one?

For a long time, I've known that many of the chemicals found in oil-based finishing and refinishing products can harm my health. Lately, the effects of wood dust have received a lot of attention, too. To get the official word on wood dust, I called my local OSHA (Occupational Safety and Health Administration) office. The industrial hygienist there told me that OSHA considers all wood dust

hazardous to health, and has recently lowered the permissible exposure levels for wood dust in the workplace. How do you know if the air in your home shop has too much wood dust? You don't, but as Dick Flynn of North Safety Equipment told me: "The bottom line is that if you're working with wood and creating dust—regardless of your collection procedures—you should always wear a respirator."

Buy a NIOSH/MSHA-approved model

All of the manufacturers I spoke with said a woodworker should settle for nothing less than a respirator jointly approved by the National Institute for Occupational Safety and Health (NIOSH) and the Mine Safety and Health Administration (MSHA). These organizations approve respirators for specific hazardous substances. For example, you need to wear a dusts/mists-approved respirator when sanding. For applying finishes, strippers, or other oil-based products, look for a gas/vapor-approved unit. Gas/vapor

respirators typically have dust/mists-approved prefilters.

With this information in mind, the large number of nonapproved dust masks on the shelves of my local hardware and discount stores startled me. For instance, the most widely sold masks—commonly labeled "nuisance masks" or "non-toxic dust masks," such as the one shown on the left in the photo at *left*—have no approval rating. Manufacturers told me they recommend these masks only for nontoxic dusts.

Cartridge-type reusable respirators: The versatile choice

Unlike disposables, reusable respirators hold interchangeable cartridges for absorbing a wide variety of pollutants. A separate prefilter as shown *opposite, top* fits on top of the cartridge for catching large particulates.

These respirators cost $20–$25 just for the facepiece (without cartridges or prefilters), but offer a cost advantage over disposables if you frequently need a respirator. For example, one change of gas/vapor pre-filters and cartridges costs $8–14, compared to about $11–$15 for equivalent disposables. Dust/mist cartridges and prefilters will cost about $4 to $5 per change.

After wearing reusable and disposable respirators from several manufacturers, I noticed that the reusables formed a slightly tighter seal against my face. Don Reycroft of North Safety Equipment agreed with my findings: "The soft silicone facepiece of reusables conforms better to facial features."

On the other hand, disposables weigh less and don't interfere with your line of sight as much as cartridge types. Since you just throw them away, you don't have to bother with cleaning disposables or changing exhalation and inhalation valves.

Reusable respirators have screw-in cartridges, prefilters, and plastic caps for holding the prefilters atop the cartridges.

The best of both worlds?

Recently, a friend in the auto-body business tipped me off to a disposable mask that costs $14 to $17, but looks and works like a cartridge-type mask. Naturally, I just had to check out his claims. Sure enough, the 3M Easi-Care paint-spray respirator shown *below* has a supple facepiece that fits as tightly as any cartridge-type respirator. Although you can't change the cartridges, you can replace the prefilters

3M's disposable Easi-Care respirator *looks like* a reusable mask, but costs just a few dollars more than other gas/vapor-approved disposables.

several times before the cartridges wear out. My distributor charges about $8 for a pack of 10 prefilters.

Disposables: The convenient choice

If you have only occasional need for a respirator, a disposable unit might be your best buy. In the past several years, throwaway respirators have become increasingly popular. When choosing a disposable, keep in mind that some models (such as the one I'm wearing on *page 78*) have exhalation valves. These one-way valves add to the cost but help reduce heat and condensation inside the mask.

For more information
• **Moldex/Metric.** Call 800-421-0668 or 213-870-9121.
• **North Safety Equipment.** Call 401-943-4400.
• **3M.** Call 800-328-1667 or 612-733-8029 for retail sources; for respirator advice, call 800-243-4630 or 612-733-6234.

Respirator Tips: How to get the most from your mask

While compiling the Survival Guide information about respirators we heard over and over from our industry sources that a respirator must be properly worn and maintained. These pointers will extend the life of your respirator and keep your lungs clear, too:

• If you have respiratory problems, such as emphysema or asthma, check with your doctor before using a respirator. Because the air-filtering components of respirators add resistance to the flow of air, your lungs have to work harder while you wear a respirator.

• Remember that cartridge-type respirators come in several sizes. Buy a mask that fits you, and return any respirator that doesn't form a tight fit around your nose and mouth.

• Even when wearing a respirator, you should properly ventilate your work area. This will reduce the chances of exposure to hazardous materials and increase the life of your respirator.

• Between uses, store a gas/vapor-approved respirator in an airtight plastic bag. Doing so will extend the life of the charcoal filters and keep the facepiece free of sawdust and other debris.

• A gas/vapor respirator has lost its effectiveness when you smell odors through it. Change cartridges in reusable masks and pitch disposables as soon as they clog or wear out.

• Even small doses of wood dust over long periods of time can cause chronic lung ailments. So, it makes sense to wear a respirator even if you're in your shop for just a short time. It doesn't pay to take chances with your health.

• Since no dust collector captures 100 percent of air-borne wood-dust particles, you should wear a respirator even when your dust collector is running.

HEARING PROTECTION— YOUR DEFENSE AGAINST SHOP NOISE

On top of everything else you hear each day, shop noise can put you over the threshold that leads to hearing loss.

Do your ears ring after you operate a whining router? That's one sign of noise-induced hearing damage. If you expose your ears too long or too frequently to sounds above their safe tolerance, you'll suffer permanent hearing loss.

In a survey of high school industrial arts teachers, the state of Iowa discovered that 54 percent had a job-related loss. Yet, only about 3 percent of the teachers surveyed said they always wore hearing protection devices in the shop. Now Iowa and other states enforce state laws requiring hearing protection for teachers *and* students.

Of course, you probably don't spend as much time in a noisy shop as an industrial arts teacher, but consider all the other loud noises you hear daily: blaring music, loud mufflers, and construction noise, for instance. They all add up. The federal Occupational Safety and Health Administration (OSHA) reports that if you exceed a level of 90 dBA (a special decibel scale for measuring noise damaging to hearing) for eight hours a day, you'll have some

permanent hearing loss. Maximum safe exposure times for other levels are shown in the table below.

Now consider the racket some of your woodworking equipment makes. From the list on this page, you'll see that a planer generates 108–118 dBA. According to OSHA, the longest your ears could take this punishment without some degree of hearing loss is about 15 minutes.

How much protection?

To safeguard your hearing you must use devices with a high enough noise reduction rating (NRR) to bring the loudest dBA level of your working equipment down to a safe plateau. Let's say, for instance, that the working planer, at an average 115 dBA, is the highest noise level you'll encounter in your shop. Reducing what you hear to a safe 90 dBA level requires ear protection devices with a minimum NRR of 25 (quality devices state their noise reduction capability on the packaging).

However, if you don't own or run a planer, or anything else approaching that noise level, ear protection devices with a lower NRR will be sufficient.

Hearing protection options

Cotton balls, an old standby, are inadequate because they cannot block dangerous intensity or frequency levels. Reliable hearing protection devices muffle and filter noise that can damage your ears, but they don't shut out all sound. Unless you've already lost hearing, you can discern a machine in operation and pick up conversation.

The chart *opposite* includes a sampling from the two categories of hearing protection devices— muffs and ear plugs. These and similar products are available from safety supply houses, large tool and hardware retailers, and mail-order woodworking suppliers. Which device you choose should depend on its NRR, its wearing comfort, and how easy it is to clean.

Inexpensive foam-type ear plugs, the choice of many home woodworkers, provide protection, ease of cleaning, and more comfort than preshaped plugs. Their life span is limited to a few washings and wearings, however, and they give you a "stopped-up" feeling. You'll also have to insert, remove, and reinsert them if you can't stand to wear them all the time.

Muffs, the other popular (but comparatively expensive) alternative, are comfortable, easy to put on and take off, and have replaceable parts. They don't give you the stopped-up sensation, but their bulk can be bothersome.

In its state recommendation to high school industrial arts teachers, Iowa suggests either of the above for shop use. We suggest you try both at a dealer's before you decide, even if you have to spend 15 cents to test the disposable plugs.

OSHA NOISE LEVEL EXPOSURE LIMITS

At this noise level	Hearing loss can occur after
85 dBA	16 hours
90 dBA	8 hours
95 dBA	4 hours
100 dBA	2 hours
105 dBA	1 hour
110 dBA	½ hour
115 dBA	15 minutes

SHOP NOISE LEVELS*

Machine	Noise generated
Planer	108–118 dBA
Jointer	103–104 dBA
Belt sander	98–99 dBA
Router	105–110 dBA
Tablesaw	96–99 dBA
Disc sander	92–93 dBA
Circular saw	103 dBA
Jigsaw	98 dBA
Hammering	94 dBA

*Tools generating over 90 dBA

HEARING PROTECTION DEVICES

TYPE	APPROX. COST	NOISE REDUCTION RATING (in decibels)	DURABILITY (with typical home shop use)	COMMENTS
Foam	15¢/pair	29–31	Days	Can be reused several times. One size fits all. conforms to ear canal. Available with neck cord. Often misplaced. Foam can deteriorate. Washable. Wearer feels "plugged up." Must depress and fit into ear. Muffles all sound.
Pod	$3.50/pair	22	Months	Convenient easy on, easy-off. Worn under chin or over head. Washable. Silicone-covered foam comfortable, but poor seal. Can be draped over neck when not in use. One size fits all. Muffles all sound.
Silicone rubber	$1/pair	26	Months	Soft, but difficult to insert. One size fits all. Small size easy to lose. Comfortable. Washable. Wearer feels "plugged up." Available with neck cord. Muffles all sound.
Cushioned muffs	$10 to $30/set	19–29	Years	NRR varies with how worn—over head, behind head, or under neck. Foam-filled pads have higher NRR. Fluid-filled pads most comfortable. Padded headband. Muffs swivel. Replaceable pads, seals, and liners on better-quality sets. Most expensive have several noise absorbing liners. All are easy-on, easy-off. Muffle all sound.

ACKNOWLEDGMENTS

Writers

George Brandsberg—Four Cornerstones of Shop Safety, pages 79–81

Emily Freeman Pinkston—Keep Safety in Sight, pages 88–91

Jim Pollock—How Safe are Your Woodworking Habits, pages 82–87

Peter J. Stephano—Spotlight on Tablesaw Safety, pages 86–87

Project Designers

Clyde Allison—Ready Wrench Rack, pages 28–29

Dave Ashe—Sit-A-Spell Shop Stool, pages 43–46

Philip Belanger—Handy Hardware Hauler, page 34

Jim Boelling—Universal Wall Cabinet System, pages 8–13; Forstner Bit Holders, page 14; Clamp Storage Extravaganza, pages 20–23; On-the-Go Glue Caddy, page 35

Bob Colpetzer—Handy Home For A Family of Pliers, page 30

James R. Downing—Universal Wall Cabinet System, pages 8–13; Sanding-Supply Organizer, pages 15–19; Clamp Storage Extravaganza, pages 20–23; Lumber Storage Rack, pages 24–27; Saw-Blade Selector, page 31; Labor of Love Workbench, pages 47–55; Workhorse of a Workbench, pages 37–42; Air-Filtration Cabinet, pages 56–60; Custom Mitersaw Cabinet, pages 61–66; Customized Tablesaw Base, pages 67–69; Router Extension Table, pages 70–71; The Ultimate Router Fence System, pages 72–75; Drill-Press Dust Collector, page 76; Swing-Arm Support, page 77

Chuck Hedlund—All-Business Bandsaw Blade Holder, pages 30–31

Kevin Heilman—Plain-Handy Plane Holder, page 33

Marlen Kemmet, Universal Wall Cabinet System, pages 8–13; Lathe Tool Rack, page 32

Raymond Russell—Quick-As-A-Wink Chisel Rack, page 28

Russell Smith—Palm-Sander Holder, page 34

Merwin Snyder—Simple Saw Rack, page 31

Richard Tollesfson—Clamp Storage Extravaganza, pages 20–23

John M. Turok—Scrollsaw Blade Organizer, page 33

Photographers

Bob Calmer
John Hetherington
Hopkins Associates
William Hopkins
Jim Kascoutas

Illustrators

James A. Downing
Jamie Downing
Kim Downing
Mike Henry
Roxanne LeMoine
Jim Stevenson
Bill Zaun

If you would like to order any additional copies of our books, call 1-800-678-2802 or check with your local bookstore.